ALBANY STREET KID

By Carmen J. Viglucci

Dedication

For those who inhabit these pages, especially those no longer with us, my mother Helen (Nell) Fitzgerald Viglucci and my father Carmen A. (Jinx) Viglucci, my brothers Mike and Andrew, my sister Helen (Honey), my many aunts and uncles on both sides of my family and 30 first cousins—plus all the other Albany street kids of the forties who in my memory will never grow old

Preface

I have had trouble finding a theme for this piece. Should I record the diverse, and often unbelievable, chronicles of two ethnic families contending with each other and at the same time with the Great Depression and/or the Big War? If conflict is the basis for literature, this would be--holy mackerel!!!.

Or it could be the simple tale of Jinx, an Italian immigrant would-be entrepreneur, and Nell, as Irish as a Fitzgerald and a Gilligan could make her, and their attempts to survive amid perhaps the greatest challenges facing young people since the Black Plague.

As it turns out, the recording of these remembrances defy style. It is not history because it is not chronological; it is not autobiography, I am not important enough for that; stream of consciousness? Nah, well, sort of; memoirs comes closest, though it includes paeans to illustrious fellow travelers, such as Amedeo Giannini, who became the world's No. 1, make that *numero uno* banker who still is no more important in this rendition than a neighborhood counterpart who was the centerpiece of the following transaction: The immigrant was buying a new pair of shoes. The clerk measured his feet as size 9 and told him they would cost $9.95. As customer Giovanni walked gingerly about, he pointed to another pair, 'And watta size those?'

The clerk checked them out, and answered, 'Twelve and a half.'

'Quanta costa?'

The clerk said, 'The same price.'

'Aha!' He waggled his finger in the air. 'I take-a the big ones!'

This is not my personal remembrance, suited to be called a memoir, but is a worthy tale of the ghetto -- be advised that ghetto is an Italian word. And that leads us to another possibility, *sociology,* a look at the Little Italy of the 1930s and 1940s typified by the battle cry, 'The South End against the world!'

Fine, but we would also have to include another part of Albany, the northern sections, where many Irish, including the Fitzgeralds, slogged their way through the depression. We could call it 'a tale of two cities .'

For the sake of facilitation, memoirs it must be.

So, if you were writing your memoirs and...

There was an older man who lived on your childhood street who was a leather-faced homosexual ward leader named Jigger who dressed like baseball's Connie Mack and managed the neighborhood baseball team, and had a wooden leg to boot, would you try to disguise him with a fabricated name, occupation and sexual preference?

If you were writing your memoirs and... You believed there often is more honor among thieves and gamblers than among priests and board chairmen, why would you think it reprehensible to use the actual names of bookies and numbers runners?

If you were writing your memoirs and... You had an Irish uncle named Dinny who might get a bit 'happy' (along with the rest of the attendees)at Great Depression family parties and recite Robert Service poems and sing 'Ace in the Hole' and 'They

Cut Down the Old Pine Tree,' would you change his name to Walter?

If you were writing your memoirs and...

You were describing the death of a close family member, would you adhere to your own memory or that of relatives who had different versions?

If you were writing your memoirs and...

A trusted friend told you of his dramatic encounter with Babe Ruth, would you omit it because there was no way to verify it?

In that vein, tell me a better name for a street kid than the real Doodles Duncan? Or, God love 'im, Big Tooth Calabro? Or Buglugs Trimarchi?

But you may wonder how did these street handles originate? The following should provide a clue:

Fourzie Calabro. During the war, the top draft classification was 1-A. With that as a guide, we decided Frankie would be 4-Z, eventually it became Fourzie.

Big Tooth Calabro. Tony had a rather prominent front tooth.

The 9 o'clock special ... Van Woert Street's Mrs. Finnegan. That was the time of night she made her last trip to

Sadie Burns' store, which closed at 10.

Monkey on a String (Lorraine Finnegan's husband). Because he was hen-pecked.

Ghost Teehan. Because of his pallor.

KO Burns from North Albany. A great street fighter.

Clubber Burns. KO's brother had a clubfoot.

Little Beaver. Little Beaver was an American sidekick of movie hero Red Ryder. Billy Joe Watso, who also was a native American, as a youngster fit the sobriquet, in our depraved minds.

Olive Oyl. Billy Joe's older, spindly sister June, who later on in life grew into an attractive young lady who would merit an entirely different kind of description.

Fatso Watso. John, the head of the Watso family was round but strong and agile.

Nuts and Bolts. A man who lived in one of the flats in the same house as the Tiger A.C. He had some kind of a mechanical job in a die factory, thus the nickname. A sidebar comment, 'He was more nuts than bolts.'

Halt, Scout, halt. On Van Woert Street, everyone was 'scout.' Nothing to do with the Boy Scouts ... we wouldn't be caught dead. When someone was telling an outlandish story or taking an unpopular comment, we would hold out our arms, hands up and say, 'Halt, Scout, halt!'

'Slivers' Willigan. He ran the numbers on Arbor Hill ... and had a wooden leg.

Bessie the Bull. She was a sizeable and stern woman who managed the Paramount Theater on Clinton Avenue.

Buglugs Trimarchi. I'm not sure what the sobriquet means, probably just enthusiast.

Doodles Duncan. Just for the sonorous alliteration

These are some of the dilemmas dogging the road to veracity in this account. Wherever possible, I have researched or used written accounts and photographic reminders to be truthful and factual. But many times there are no records. Often, honest witnesses to the same event remember it entirely differently. Here I follow my own recollections if I have any. If I only have hearsay knowledge, I will defer to someone who was on the scene. If there is no way to ascertain the actuality, I, eagerly, accept the most intriguing version.

Truth really is stranger than fiction so I would find it not only wrong but foolish to make something up when the facts are handy.

I have learned something else. There is a reality which supersedes truth or legend! When you grow up in a neighborhood full of story-tellers and poets and adventurers, of hard-hearted nuns and loving whores, you learn that things are hardly ever what they seem. That there is another kind of truth than facts.

I will go to lengths to avoid embarrassing people, many of whom have not had the mental or social blessings or wherewithal to escape public ridicule. In the case of a sixth grader whose less-than-average intelligence drew the ridicule of a teaching nun, I have changed his name ... but not hers.

When the most important personage who ever visited your school is Mr. Peanut, you learn to elevate surreal above real.

Chapter 1
Holy Day

Aug. 15, 1950. It was the day the Roman Catholic Church proclaimed it a matter of faith that the Blessed Mother had been assumed bodily into Heaven -- it was to be a holy day of obligation (you had to go to Mass or else). This proclamation was made at Vatican City by Pope Pius XII amid centuries-weathered pomp and panoply, Gregorian chanting brushed with the most intense incense, processions coming and going, all witnessed by thousands of pilgrims.

For all his worldly stature and esteem, this pope, Pius XII, was more like us than he was akin to the Blessed Mother; witness his love for driving fast cars or his favorite song, 'Ciribiribin,' as recorded by Harry James.

Father Richard P. McBrien in his two-volume book 'Catholicism,' describes it this way: 'The Assumption was not merely a personal privilege conferred upon Mary but a reality bestowed in view of her role in the economy of salvation, so the Assumption is not merely a personal privilege unrelated to the wider mission of her life 'her call to final union with God in Christ, in the totality of her human existence (body and soul) was also unique in the end.'

With explanations like that who needs mysteries!

This first Assumption Day got off to a much more profane start at 286 Clinton Avenue, where a man was to die who was not to be assumed bodily into heaven. The night before that man passed away, he, my father, was at the kitchen table in the basement when I arrived home late. He wasn't feeling just right and asked me to work for him in the morning but I begged off. We were running the family business, the State News, downtown at 132 State Street, in the shadow of the State Capitol in Albany, New York. Later, brother Andrew came home and agreed to open up at 6 a.m. Thus, I was still sleeping when Mother woke me about 7:30 a.m. 'Come downstairs, something's wrong with your father.' Then, she called up to brother Mike on the top floor who hadn't yet left for work. Mike and his wife Ann and their two young sons, Andy and

Mikey, lived on the top floor of the three-story rowhouse. The rest of us -- Mother, Daddy, Andrew, sister Honey, grandfather Pop and I, shared the basement and first floor.

As Mother, Mike and I headed to the bedroom next to the kitchen, Mother explained:

"I was doing laundry and when I went by the bedroom I saw him sitting on the edge of the bed with his pants half on. I was folding clothes for a while when I realized he hadn't come out. When I looked again, he was like that ..."

She pointed to Daddy slumped on the floor next to the bed. It took Mike and me all our strength to lift him onto the bed. Someone phoned Dr. Derkowski and soon he was on the scene.

'Will someone come here for a minute?' he called from the bedroom. Mike was comforting Mother who was crying and wringing her hands. Honey was scared to death. So I went in.

'Get on the other side of him,' the doctor motioned to where the bed was against the wall, 'and hold his head up ... like this.' I had an arm under Daddy's head and, when the doctor gave him an injection in the arm, he threw up, but it didn't seem to be vomit. It was like pinkish foam and it was copious.

'That's got to be good, doesn't it?' I said as I clambered out from the bed.

'Yes,' the doctor said low.

Out in the kitchen, I pronounced, 'Things are better. He threw up and the doctor said that's good.'

Mother would not be calmed though Mike was doing his best. The doctor came into the kitchen and asked, 'Are you his wife?'

'Yes,' Mother answered.

'Then you'll have to sign the death certificate.'

My heart dropped.

His body didn't rise through the sunny August morning but I always felt Daddy went straight to heaven; that he had paid his dues here.

(Dear reader: Brother Mike's version of this tragic ending differs somewhat from mine but since I was an eyewitness, you are stuck with my account).

I called Andrew at the State News; that was a difficult call. But there is a strange excitement in those morbid calls.

Cousin Mickey Regan showed up shortly after to help me weather the moment and we went to Duke's Place on Hudson Avenue and had hot dogs with 'everything on them.' Duke's frankfurter sauce drew adherents from far and wide.

That evening, my high school friend Bob Sweeney telephoned and said, 'Let's go somewhere. You have to get out.'

Bob knew family tragedy. One bright, summer day, his father excused himself from the Sunday dinner table in Gloversville, calmly went out on the front porch and shot himself in the head.

Mr. Sweeney owned one or more glove factories in Gloversville (where else?), about 25 miles from Albany. If Edward Arlington Robinson hadn't already concocted 'Richard Corey,' Mr. Sweeney could have had been the prototype.

I looked forward to Bob Sweeney's company. Though he drank a bit for his age he was mature, and I don't mean Victor. He knew the ropes. We went to play miniature golf at (the)Patio on Central Avenue. Exciting, huh? But it served the purpose.

Chapter 2
Dust to Dust

Wakes still took place at the decedent's home when Carmen 'Jinx' Viglucci, our 'Daddy,' died on the new Holy Day of Obligation when Mary, the other mother in our lives, rose into heaven, body and soul. When I heard that phrase, it reminded me of the film noir masterpiece, 'Body and Soul,' starring John Garfield and Lilli Palmer, and also the song of the same name, made famous by the great saxophonist Coleman Hawkins.

The funereal event, Jinx's, not Blessed Mary's, was proclaimed by a black wreath affixed on the front door at 286 Clinton. Daddy was laid out in the living room just on the other side of the sliding pocket doors of the bedroom I shared with Pop, my grandfather.

The first night of the wake when everyone else was asleep, I went into the living room. I had been wondering how the crease of his pants stood up so stiffly. I looked under the pants leg and found newspapers stuffed inside. Observe and learn, Leonardo had advised.

Many came to say goodbye to Jinx who himself had come a long way from his birth site in the tiny stucco house back in the Appenine hills of Bellona, not far from the city of Caserta in Italy.

The roll call:

His own family, wife Helen, called Nell by some, particularly by her husband; his four children, Mike, Andrew, Carmen, and the youngest, Honey, 14, and their retinue of youngish friends. To keep the record clear, we called our father 'Daddy,' and always referred to our mother as just that-- 'Mother.'

Daddy was also survived by his mother, Carmela (known as Zi' Carmel in her South End neighborhood) two sisters, Giuseppina and Genevieve, and their grown children.

Then there were the Fitzgeralds -- his in-laws -- too numerous for accounting. Some loved Jinx, particularly Margaret Regan, our living-saint aunt; some were impressed less favorably -- Aunt Mary Waters, who often referred to him as 'little Caesar.'

Except for a few quirks and wrinkles, these groups were not too different from those at any wake for a 48-year-old man with family.

But Jinx -- it would have pleased him to read this -- was not an ordinary man. He also had moved in offbeat circles and the friends, cronies, associates, gamblers, drinkers, debtors, creditors came not to praise or bury Jinx, but to make required tributes; there are also earthly days of obligation.

Ames O'Brien, who ran numbers for Dan O'Connell, the Dems' political boss, in the north part of Albany, asked brother Mike if there were enough cars for the funeral. 'Could always use some,' Mike supposed. 'Let me take care of it,' the well-dressed Ames said softly. He did. The next day, five or six unexpected autos with drivers joined the funeral cortege when it left St. Anthony's in the South End to wend its way to St. Agnes Cemetery, Albany's principal Roman Catholic burial ground, in the suburb of Menands.

Also making the roll call was a downtowner who remained in the hallway outside the open door to the living room, which was Jinx's final domiciliary resting place.

Dapper in a fedora, the man paying his respects spread his suit jacket just wide enough to reveal the 'piece' in a holster draped over his shoulder. He said, 'That's the way it goes, kid.' Circling one hand in the air over his fedora, he continued, 'You're in the whirl, in the whirl, and then suddenly you're out of the whirl ...' his hand flung open to one side in emphasis. 'Well, good luck to the family and, well, you know, God bless and all that.'

Proper civilities rendered, he turned on an elevated heel and left.

Chapter 3
Forget Naples!

A famous saying glorifies the city of
Naples in southern Italy, 'Vede Napoli, e
poi muori!' 'See Naples and then die!'
Daddy had a different viewpoint:
'Someday, somewhere, somebody is going
to tell you that you should go to Italy ... it's
beautiful,' Jinx said. He was at the kitchen
table in his A-style tee-shirt and
suspenders, using his thumb and
fingertips to twirl the tiny curls at the side
of his otherwise bald head. He interrupted
his work at the crossword puzzle.
'Don't believe them.' He leaned forward.
'It's lousy. And the Bay of Naples stinks!'
He actually bared his teeth to make the
point and I had to resist staring at the gold
tooth in the front of his mouth.
'OK,' I accepted his remark. 'Were you
from Naples, Daddy?'
'Nah. Thank God.'
'Where then?' I pushed on.
'Nowhere worth talking about,' he said. He
got up and pulled his suspenders down
over his arms and began putting on his

shirt.

'Yeah, but ...'

'No yeah-buts,' he said in that voice made gravelly by chronic asthma. 'Case closed.' He re-adjusted his suspenders and then slipped on his arm-bands, sliding his sleeves up under them to fit his short arms.

'But,' I tried one more time. He was already half out the back door, waving his hand back at me in a 'forget it' gesture. The encounter ... confrontation ... took place probably in the summer of 1946 when we lived on Van Woert Street in Albany's North End proper ... 'proper' because there was also North Albany, a settlement of lace curtain Irish farther up the pike but also part of the city of Albany. Little did we know at the time that Jinx had only a couple of years left to disparage the homeland of Virgil, Cicero, Dante, Giotto, Francis of Assisi, Catherine of Siena, Julius Caesar, Thomas Aquinas, Pirandello, Leonardo DaVinci, Michelangelo, Raffaelo, Machiavelli, and, uh, Joe DiMaggio.

Not to mention such foreigners as Keats, Byron, Shelly, Thomas Mann, Mark Twain

and others who revealed their passions for Italy in other tongues. And, of course, the Forefathers of The good ole USA.
Uh oh, only one female ... well, how about Sophia Loren? She did win the Academy Award for 'Two Women' in 1960. And we could add Silvana Mangano, Anna Magnani and Giulietta Masini. And while we are on the subject of notable women, we must remember such non-Italians as St. Teresa of Lisieux, the Teresa from Avila, Mother Teresa of Calcutta, and, of course, Mother Machree! All of whom undoubtedly would have kind words to say about bella Italia.

Chapter 4
Fond Farewell

Daddy had been across the ocean twice by the time he was five years old. It was something he never talked about, just as he seldom ever mentioned the Old Country except in derogatory terms.

Not too many years ago, one could look through the telephone books anywhere in the world --and that includes the United States and Italy -- and you would rarely ever find the name Vigliucci (or even the Americanized Viglucci).

Yet in that tiny village of Bellona, Italy, there are two family lines with the name Vigliucci -- and they are not related. Both have been coming their separate ways for hundreds of years and they claim no connection.

Bellona, from where our 'genitori' emigrated early in the 20th century, is in farm country -- tobacco and peaches are rich but the people are poor. This poverty in 1904 led Michele Vigliucci and Carmela Aurilio, from the contiguous village of Vitulazio, to pack up some belongings and, taking their little girl Giuseppina and their 2-year-old Carmine, somehow to make the 50-mile trek, maybe on foot, to the bittersweet Santa Lucia waterfront on the Golfo di Napoli. The haunting song, "Santa Lucia," captures the emotions felt by the southern Italians heading for America as they looked back for the last time at their homeland then turned West to the Statue of Liberty. Most stare in trepidation, make the Sign of the Cross, and blink away a tear or two before heading to the unknown New World. I imagine my father, at 2, giving Santa Lucia, bay and saint, the traditional Italian arm gesture in farewell. Michele, my grandfather DaDa, had been born in the same bed as his father and his son at the blue stucco house at 49 Via Santa Maria degli Angeli in Bellona. Giuseppina and Carmine also were born in that big double bed in a room whose little balcony opened to a wide and panoramic view of the southern Italian countryside. The best things in life truly are free if you prefer scenery to steak.

Right or wrong, that simple birthright was left behind for the dream of a better lifestyle. One can easily imagine little

Carmine nervously jiggling the padlock on the courtyard gate as the family left forever, headed for an uncertain fate. DaDa was listed as 'contadina' (peasant) on Carmine's birth certificate. Never was there a more unlikely peasant farmer's son than my father.

Flash-ahead

Now, you may ask, if our father was so reticent about his background, how are all these homeland facts popping up' Many years later, this author, with my wife (nee Costa) Patricia, (Trish to me and you, too), managed to unearth daddy's hometown.

We were on a tour guided by the superb Antonio Parisi and were approaching heavenly Naples. I told him about Daddy and asked if he had ever heard of Bellona. He hadn't but that night contacted a cab driver friend and sadly reported back that no such town could be found in the area. We were disappointed but not for long. The cabdriver later said he had indeed found a Bellona but near Caserta. We, along with Trish's father Sam Costa, Antonio and the cab-driver, Carmine

Monetti, met in the Piazza Sasso in Sorrento and agreed on terms of the trip which was to take off the next morning. Just Trish and I would go with the taxi driver who auspiciously was named Carmine as was his father.

On the way we passed by Castellamare di Stabia. Our driver who by now was on the verge of cousinhood, said the little seaside town had become famous as a refuge of the exiled American mobster Vito Genovese.

Perhaps to get the bad taste out of our mouths, Carmine quickly said, 'I also once was guide to Mario Cuomo searching for family members'

It took less than two hours before we spotted the sign 'Bellona' in the countryside off the Autostrada di Sole. We received refined directions from a road crew and soon were in the main piazza of Bellona. Carmine parked and left us in the car as he went into the village church to gather information. As we sat I noticed a monument to the town's war dead. My eyes automatically skimmed to the bottom of the alphabetically-arranged sign--there they were, 'Vigliucci Michele, fu Andrea.'

God bless 'em! This was the place!
Vigliucci is the correct spelling for our last name; the second 'i' was discarded at Ellis Island.
Then Carmine returned a bit less excited than Trish and I.
'It seems there are two families Vigliucci and they are not related. But they told me the address for one of them. ' Shall we?'
He spread his hands in front of him, his head cocked to one side.
We drove to a small home at 13 Piazza Dante Alighieri. Carmine went to a door at the side of the house and soon was rushing back to us with a ruddy-faced Vigliucci 'This is them,' Carmine was shouting, 'These are your Vigliuccis!'
The Prodigal Son had come home with wife!
Accompanying our chauffeur, you guessed it, was Andrea, who was about the same age as brother Andrew! As best as I can figure he was a rather close relative -- maybe a second cousin. Soon, Vigliuccis were popping up from everywhere. Cabdriver Carmine, as is the wont of Italians, became an instant 'cugino.' The celebration lasted for hours; we only left

because we had to re-join our tour. That night, guide Antonio summed it up neatly: 'You are not seeing where your ancestors lived. You yourself are in reality returning home.'

Take that, Daddy. I raised my eyes above. That visit opened the doors to other family now living in England, and in Belgium. Indeed not too long after I received a beautiful letter from one Lina Pancaro, a resident of Hyde, England, near Manchester, the daughter of Raffaela, nee Vigliucci married to Giacomo Pancaro. We also came to know Lina's sister Antonietta and husband Raff DelGiudice; brother Peter Pancaro and his wife Christine from the Emerald Isle, as well as varied and sundry cousins, nieces and nephews. Wouldn't Jinx have been thrilled!?

Chapter 5
Land of Milk and Cupcakes

A couple of years later in Albany when my grandmother became pregnant, out of distrust for things American, she went back to Italy, only temporarily, to have her third child, Genevieve. For whatever reason, Grandma took little Carmine back and forth with her before settling down in Albany for good in 1907.

That five-year-old whose Atlantic voyage time rivaled that of Christopher Columbus grew up to be 'Jinx' Viglucci, cab driver, newspaper circulation manager, entrepreneur, bar owner, newsstand owner, and Italianaphobe -- even to the point of not allowing his children to learn the language.

Let Jinx tell it:

'When I came over the second time -- I was about five -- my Uncle Andrew took me to the Waldorf cafeteria at State and Pearl. Pointing at a glass of milk and a chocolate cupcake he bought me, he said, 'This is America, not back on Grand Street where you live ... this is where you should be, not there.'

Daddy recounted this in perfect English; the only sign of his immigrant status was mispronouncing such words as desks ('desk-es') and follow ('folly')and using the non-word 'irregardless.'

Anyway, he took to heart the kind of advice his uncle proffered because most of his career endeavors were to take place in the environs of State and Pearl, a corner to be referred to by some public relationist in later years as 'the crossroads of the great Northeast.'

It was near there as a boy that he earned the nickname which was to follow him throughout his life. Brother Andrew relates the story in Bill Kennedy's 'O, Albany!' :

'All kids were put out to work at an early age. My father started to work at age six, selling papers at Union Station. The older paperboys didn't like him and named him Jinx, this cute little kid selling papers. People would ignore the big kids and buy his papers and give him a fifty-cent piece.'

I wish Daddy had stayed around longer. I have no idea, for instance, at how he would react to being the subject of a Pulitzer Prize author.

'Napolitan' Holiday

Surely, there was a lot to be said for Waldorf cafeteria chocolate cupcakes as well as that cafeteria's baked macaroni and cheese and its chili. But, obviously its culinary capabilities could hardly compare to the delicacies of Zi' Carmela's 'cucina.' We Viglucci and LoGiudice cousins shared the common belief of almost all Italian kids: 'My grandma is the greatest cook in the world.'

Hey, that acclaim without question is justified in each and every case. The time, the effort, the expertise, and, yes, the love, should never be forgotten. But does anyone else but I find such praise just a bit overdone, like macaroni cooked beyond 'al dente'? Has anyone noticed the vacant look on the faces of the grandkids as we describe for the thousandth time the dandelion soup with the just perfect little meatballs? Certainly grandma's feasts were almost beyond belief but in the recounting, do we run roughshod over the sensibilities of good friends of other nationalities or persuasions?

With that said, let me relate that routine Sunday fare at 81 Grand Street would include macaroni ('pasta' was used to paper walls). Spaghetti was popular but mostly we had long, tubular macaroni, often home-made. Chicken was usually the game of choice, which is easily said but not easily prepared.

Grandma would begin the process on Saturday when she and her cohorts would descend on the public market, about three blocks away, and hand-pick live chickens. Grandma would crate hers home where she would execute it in her own strong hands by wringing its neck over the kitchen sink. She would boil the feathers away, clean it, cut it up and otherwise prepare for the next day's dinner where part of it would flavor the sauce.

Noon dinner would also include salad, home-made bread or a loaf or two from Rossano's bakery across the street. If we had dessert, it probably would be fried dough sprinkled with sugar, which we called, in the Napolitan dialect, 'ee-wand' more commonly known as 'wandi.' All washed down with plenty of wine 'originale,' of course, thank you, DaDa.

Kids were offered wine, too, but usually preferred soda -- orange or grape.

The younger set would consist generally of Mike, Andrew, myself, and Honey along with the LoGiudice cousins, Connie, Joe, Mela, and Sammy who were fun company. A fifth sibling, Mary Ann, arrived too late for the 81 Grand Sundays. Also, cousin Frances, who lived with Grandma since the family breakup. Augie had gotten married and moved off to Washington, D.C, for an exotic lifestyle.

The LoGiudices' parents were my gracious Aunt Gen and Uncle Sam. Neighbors also would be on hand, indicating that Grandma was indeed the cook we thought she was. Most fascinating was Tess, the white witch, who would assure that all the food was pure and safe.

This basic Sunday dinner would be the model for the most important day of the year, Easter Sunday, which would be enhanced by more of everything and the addition of dandelion soup with the tastiest small meatballs, chocolate bunnies, and on at least one occasion, a thick cream pie from one of the Grand Street bakeries.

The Sunday repast and its leftovers would also establish the menu for the next few days.

I have many reasons for writing these memoirs, not the least the fact that my brothers, sister and I had the unusual background of having been brought up for long periods in the homes of both set of grandparents. We lived for some five years in one of the apartments in my grandmother's building in the South End and then for some more than 10 years in Pop's house on Van Woert Street. Undoubtedly we were closer to Mother's family because we lived directly with them and for a longer period. Some years back, I was asked what was Irish cooking like. At the height of my stupidity, I answered there was no such thing as Irish cuisine. Fact is that I hadn't seen the trees for the forest.

Let's face it; we were Irish and we ate food -- that made it Irish food! I think the Irish traditions could be found in fish cakes 'bits of cod cooked in potato cakes or onions sliced up and put in the hamburger meat before cooked.'

And though we never recognized it as a

national dish, lamb stew quite often was served.

We definitely ate potato cakes with caraway seeds and Mother made 'potato puffs,' stirring eggs in the mashed spuds, then sautéing , as Monday leftovers. Sure, and we ate cabbage on the saint's day, mostly with ham but also with corned beef. And don't forget the yellow split pea soup, a favorite to this day.

Ham also assumed prominence on Easter morn when, following Big Tim's lead, we were allowed as many eggs as we could stuff down.

And it is to be noted that we frequently had fried cornmeal mush. A dish prominent in both Irish and Italian kitchens. Think about it.

Another hot breakfast item which found its way to the U.S. from Eire was oatmeal. When cousin Augie lived with Grandma across the hall at 81 Grand, he often would tap lightly at our door in the morning and he considered the oatmeal Mother would serve him as Irish. It undoubtedly was more filling than the bowl of cafe -latte Grandma served every day with crusty bread.

Perhaps the most Irish of our meals was served Fridays, creamed codfish with boiled potatoes. Another Irish probability was boiled onions and vegetable soups wouldn't be considered soups without barley.

Chapter 6

Gospel According to Dennis

About the time Zi' Andrea and Carminucc' (phonetically Car-min-ooch), soon to be known as Jinx, were chasing down cupcakes with milk at State and Pearl, Tim and Delia Fitzgerald were rearing a still increasing brood of children about three miles farther north on Pearl Street, near Colonie Street, on the other end of the city; make that world, from Grand Street. In 1852, the Fitzgeralds had come to America from County Offaly, where the lack of the staple potatoes and the abundance of religious bigotry had literally forced them out of their homeland to seek American food and shelter.

The Fitzgerald family expert genealogist, Dennis Fitzgerald, begotten of Dennis, begotten of Timothy, begotten of Dennis, has prepared a very detailed and loving account of 'the hunger' in Ireland.

Let the Dennis gospel, beginning in the mid-19th century, explain the times:

Poverty and hunger were prevalent in Ireland for centuries. A lack of raw

*materials, investment capital and a skilled
labor force had resulted in a total reliance
on agriculture. Very few Catholic farmers
owned their own farms. The Penal Laws of
1734 created a 'Protestant Ascendancy,' a
system of Protestant landlords because
Catholics were banned by law from
purchasing land or bequeathing it to their
descendants. Gradually, all the land passed
to Protestant landlords, who often resorted
to eviction and forceful removal from
houses and farms.*

*John Fitzgerald and his growing family
were desperately fighting to survive as
tenant farmers in the crown estate of
Kilconcourse in the midlands of Ireland, in
the Kinnity parish in Offaly County. Leases
for a 21-year term had been granted to
tenant farmers beginning in 1829, when
John was about 19. The tenant farmers
apparently met their rent payments
regularly ... then the potato famine came,
beginning in 1846 ... the period from 1845
to 1855 is called 'The Great Hunger' and
left over one million men, women and
children - including John's namesake - dead
from starvation, malnutrition and disease
that included typhus, dysentery and*

cholera.

Dennis' research showed that his Fitzgerald forbears by 1850 were unable to make the rent and found themselves among the surplus population ... *the Crown decided that it was cheaper to send the poor people to America than it was to support them in a poor house. The cost to keep a person in a poor house for one year was seven pounds, three shillings per year. A ticket to Boston, New York or Philadelphia was four pounds, and children were half price.*

Thus, John Fitzgerald, 42, and his wife Ellen Spain, 30, their sons Dennis, 12, Thomas, 8, and daughter Margaret, 10, found themselves boarding the sailing vessel Sarah Louisa in Liverpool England, June 11, 1852, according to biographer Dennis. *For seven long weeks, the ship would sail west.*

Also aboard, were Biddy and Catherine Spain, probably Ellen's sisters. The ship landed in New York on July 31, 1852. The Fitzgerald family settled among fellow Irish emigres in Troy where Dennis met and eventually married Mary Ellen Sweeney on Oct. 26, 1865. Dennis was on leave from the

Army in which he served during the Civil War.

Their first child was Mary, historian Dennis has reported.

A son, Timothy Edward Fitzgerald, (editor's note: later to become the legendary Pop, grandfather to some 30 of us, of many shades and nationalities) *was born on Oct. 8, 1878.* (Pop at a much later date puts all of us into familial focus when he said, 'I never imagined I would become head of my own United Nations'.)

But the family lost their first-born, who died in February of 1880. Another son, James, was born in December of the same year.

Tragically, just two years later, Dennis reported, *the Sarah Louisa went missing with all hands.*

Chapter 7
Dakota-tested

Tim's sister, the redoubtable Aunt Anne, born in 1885 after the family's return from the Dakota Territory to the comparative civilization of Troy, in later years would repeat one of the unwelcome frontier experiences probably told her by her mother Mary Ellen:

'At night the Indians would stand outside our windows and laugh at us -- they thought our clothes and cooking and eating were hilarious. Of course, they were probably harmless but it was too nerve-wracking to take the chance they would never do something crazy because they were always drunk.'

Aunt Anne, a lifelong teetotaler, may have inherited from her mother the uncanny knack for spotting drunks. She, too, could spot an inebriate from 200 yards at night even if it were an Indian on the pitch-black Dakota prairie. As the years were to pass, family members would give her ample opportunity to put this talent to use.

Anyway, *they returned to Troy in 1883. Tim Fitzgerald and Delia Gilligan* -- she was simply Ma to us kids -- *exchanged wedding vows at Sacred Heart Church in North Albany on Oct. 17, 1897. In 1899 their star-crossed son was born -- John, the second of their ten children. Mary was the first, then John, followed by James, Margaret, Helen, Timothy, Nancy, Elizabeth, Dennis, and Catherine.*

In the meanwhile, family biographer Dennis, with a sense of pride and sentiment, writes that *on Jan. 13, 1881, pilgrim Ellen Spain Fitzgerald, in her 67th year of life, occupation 'keeping house,' died. She had endured abject poverty in Ireland, had been evicted from her homeland, made a harrowing ocean voyage, buried at least three of her children, and nurtured her family to a new start in a new country'*

Then her husband, John Fitzgerald, died of 'old age' (74) in 1896.

Their son Dennis, Civil War veteran, former resident of the Dakota Territory, Troy foundry worker, suffered a sudden and shocking death on April 13, 1906. Dennis cited the Albany Times Union report: *'A distressing fatality occurred in the northern section of the City this morning when Dennis J. Fitzgerald, of 13 Van Woert Street, was run down and killed by the cars. Fitzgerald was employed as bugger and polisher at the Copinton Foundry of Troy, and at an early hour was about to board a Troy local when he stepped directly in front of an Express train and was crushed.'* Geneaologist Dennis' narrative went on: *His widow Mary Ellen lived with his widowed sister Margaret Fay at 69 Van Woert Street. Margaret worked for the O'Connell family who owned and operated the saloon at Van Woert and Broadway. The two women lived together and died within weeks of each other in February, 1916, Margaret of myocarditis and Mary Ellen of apoplexy, on Feb. 2 and 27 respectively.*

So it has been recorded that long before 1907 when Jinx Viglucci was five, his father-in-law-to-be, Tim, as a toddler and his parents and infant brother James, had already tested living in the Dakota Territory, where they may have given rise to the expression 'unhappy campers.'

Historian Dennis backgrounds the territory: *The north and south Dakota region, which after 1861, had been known as the Dakota Territory, later divided in 1889.'*

Helen, our mother, was born in the summer of 1905 probably while Daddy was, how should we put it? abroad once again.

Pop, or Pops, as Tim was later to be known in and out of family, worked as a presser at the Arrow shirtworks in Troy before moving to North Pearl Street in Albany. After North Pearl, Tim and family moved around often, in the same neighborhood, including lower Van Woert Street (so-called because it was on the other side of the mainline of the New York Central). If streets have human characteristics, then Van Woert Street would be judged schizophrenic -- both ends were on 'the other side of the tracks,' according to where one was residing at the time.

Anyway, Tim and family lived for a while on lower Van Woert near Broadway, then moved across the tracks (North Pearl Street) to No. 98, Van Woert Street proper, between Swan and Lark. The street ran east and west, a valley idyllically hilled on the south by the Colonie Street city dump and on the north by Dudley Park, one-time home to a famed observatory.

At this time, Pop was working as a cook on the Barge Canal. Once, coming home from a stretch on the boats, as he strode up Van Woert Street, his pack over his back, he heard a female voice calling to him from a second-floor window, 'Whitey ... Whitey ...' He looked up and an embarrassed woman said, 'Oh, I'm sorry, I thought you were Whitey Goldberg.'

'No, ma'm, I'm not Whitey,' Pop smiled, 'but I sure wish I was.'

Blue-eyed Dagoes

Mother said that before she and Daddy were married, Aunt Anne advised her against it.

'Don't do it, Helen,' a worried Aunt Anne remonstrated, 'marry him and the next thing you know, you'll have a bunch of little dagoes running around the house.' As usual, Aunt Anne was right. Mike was born in 1924, Andrew in 1928, Carmen in 1932, and Honey in 1936 -- all blond and blue-eyed as most 'dagoes' are.

And, Aunt Anne, at least, had the good grace not to call us 'wops,' a more pejorative term.

Chapter 8
Brotherly Discipline

Every Sunday we -- Mike, Andrew, Honey,
and I -- had to go to Grandma's for dinner
which lasted from noon to twoish. Daddy
and Mother didn't go with us any more ...
it was our obligation but no longer theirs.
And we walked there. And the fact that we
always called it 'Grandma's' tells plenty
about the power structure at the house. In
no context, did I ever hear 81 Grand Street
referred to as DaDa's.

It was about a three-mile hike from our
house on Van Woert Street, over Swan
Street, through Arbor Hill, left on Clinton
to Hawk Street, right on the bridge, which
was almost to the halfway point to
Grandma's in the South End.

Though long, the walk most of the time
was uneventful, except for crossing the
infamous Hawk Street Viaduct, from
which at that time quite a few Albanians
had purposely taken headers. Albany also
has the Northern Boulevard viaduct,
traversing the same chasm about a half-
mile west, but for some reason jumpers
ignored that span. The Hawk Street

structure   was the first cantilever arch bridge in the world.

The 'viadock,' Albany's word for it, took traffic from Clinton Avenue to Elk Street over the top of such streets as Orange, Sherman, and Sheridan, named for Albany native General Philip Sheridan). Also beneath was The Bay, one of the city's many neighborhood ballfields.

One bright Sunday, about 11 a.m., or so, probably 1941 -- because Mike would be in the Navy by 1942, the four of us were crossing the viaduct and Mike, nettled by someone's slow pace, took corrective action. Grabbing little sister Honey by her ankles, he dangled the cute 4-year-old over the railing. I can see him now, Lucky Strike dangling from his 17-year-old lips, calmly holding our screaming -- and swinging -- sister, garbed in her Sunday best dress.

'From now on you'll walk fast,' he said.

Yes, we would.

To ascertain that his command was understood, he then ordered,

'Okay, you two, dance!'

After making sure we heard right, Andrew and I began dancing in place, not rhythmically but as fast as we could. There we were, one 8, the other 12, thin blond hair flying about, feet jigging as fast as they could, hearts pounding even faster.

'I'm not taking any more crap, understand?'

'Yeah, Mike, yeah, yeah.'

Then slowly he drew her back up, gently setting our crying sister on the almost terma firma of the Hawk Street viaduct. 'Okay, Hon?' he asked solicitously, giving us one more dirty look as if it were all our fault. 'And if anybody ... anybody ... ,' looking directly at each of us in turn, 'ever says anything, I'll drop her the next time.' He had made his point. Any time after that on the Sunday walk to the South End, all Mike had to do was give a reasonable impersonation of 'that' look on his face, and we all fell into quick-stepping line. I guess you could it call brotherly discipline. The odd part of this unusual situation was I don't believe I or brother Andrew were ever really terrified; we knew Mike would never, ever hurt our sister. I'm not sure Andrew and I were that safe though-- just joking.

A Good Man

Some years later, the family's beloved
'Pop,' Tim Fitzgerald, victimized by
'senility,' passed away at the house on
Beverly Avenue off Northern Boulevard,
at the age of 82. He died in his bedroom
after refusing the last rites offered by a
scared, sweating young priest.
'I just don't know what to do,' the priest
said exasperatedly to Mother standing
there, wringing her arms desperately.
Now, within the space of ten years, she
had stood by twice in a kitchen as the two
most important men in her life died on the
other side of a wall.
In the interim between the time the body
was taken from the house and would re-
appear at the funeral parlor, Aunt Gen
brought my Italian grandmother to the
house.
Grandma had never been to our house
before -- indeed, until then, I had never
seen Grandma anywhere else in the entire
world except on Grand Street.
Away from her own turf, her tininess was
emphasized. The tough old woman, now

in her 80s, sensed that everyone was taken by her presence there, wondering what were her thoughts. Tears were in her eyes but she didn't cry or even sob when she explained, 'Tim ... was a gooda man.'

Mystery Man

In tracing the Vigliucci family tree, one name keeps popping up ' Uncle Andrew, though he was largely unseen. The family is riddled with Andrews, or Andreas, even in recent times even an Andres, Hispanic son of my brother Andrew who was married to Sara Munoz of Puerto Rico. Just to keep the record straight, the marriage did not last, and brother Andrew was to have a second wife, also Hispanic, Betsy Lopez.

With all these Andrews, we for some reason have always been aware of a particular 'Uncle Andrew.' It seems he was our grand-uncle, uncle of my father.

The existence of this shadowy relative is indirectly verified by the account of my father, as a boy, eating at a Waldorf Restaurant with his 'Uncle Andrew' who gave him the advice that led him to being an Italianaphobe and which shaped forever our family life.

Perhaps, there were so many Andrews -- and Michaels-- in the family we apparently were confused into imagining more Andrews that there actually were. For instance, there has been anecdotal mention of perhaps another 'Uncle Andrew.' It could be the same avuncular presence as noted or another Andrew. Either my mother or my father told me that at least two Vigliucci brothers or cousins, or a combination thereof, arrived in this country in the early 1900s; that something dire happened back in Bellona where their mother as part of a family business made 'caning.' Someone reportedly robbed the lady of her working machinery and refused to return it. No Vigliucci worthy of the name would stand for this insult --or it might be that the business was flourishing. As it was told to me, the new Americans went to Grant's downstreet, bought a baseball bat (befittingly in line with their new national persona). They went home(Bellona) and 'brained' the responsible person or persons.

Antonietta (Toni) Pancaro DelGiudice of Hyde, England, whose mother Raffaella was a Vigliucci, is a native of Bellona, but had no knowledge of the violence. But she did have had information lending credence to the tale: 'The family made a living from weaving long grasses (collected from the mountainside) into ropes, mats and a narrow string rope for sewing the mats which were then sold at markets.'

There is still another and possibly related family incident that a Vigliucci, again an Andrew, was involved in a knife fight in the South End of the city, in which someone was killed. The story goes that the neighborhood immigrants hid the man on their rooftops until enough money could be collected to send him back to Italy.

Which parent left me the story?' Knowing which one might lend credence to whether it happened at all. And their different genetic backgrounds give obvious hints. Helen was as Irish as any Fitzgerald could be; she knew a good story when she heard one. And how and why would anyone with the same heritage as F. Scott Fitzgerald keep such a tale buried. Jinx and his family, on the other hand, would have every reason to keep it secret. And an item from the Italian Book of Proverbs should be cited in that it also brings in the thought of burial -- 'When a man sets out to kill another, he should dig two graves--one for his victim, the other for himself.'

FYI -- A check of Albany city directories shows that, beginning in 1915, several Vigliucci men ' Michele, Andrew, Luca, Giuseppe, Nicola and Daniel ' lived at Dongan Avenue and Bleecker Street addresses.

Chapter 9
Family Break-up
When he was a young man, Jinx was coming home late from work one night. As he trudged up the stone steps at 81 Grand, at the corner of Elm Street, he noticed a car, its motor running, parked a little farther down the street, near his sister's house.

He slid into the dark doorway and watched.

'It was kind of misty,' he said. 'A woman, I knew it was Josephine, (Giuseppina)came out of the house carrying a child. Strange ... I realized in a flash what was happening ... she was running away from Frank.

'At first, I thought I should do something. But then I knew it was probably the best thing for her. She got into the car and it sped off. I stood there in the dark wondering which child she took, which one she left behind.'

Jinx's sister Josephine was married to Frank Martello, according to Mother a sinister, cruel, minor Mafioso.

'He constantly smoked those Italian cigars,' Mother said, referring to Parodi's and De Nobile's. 'He used to have his Black Hand, in Italian 'Mano Nero,' cronies to the house for card games and they treated Josephine like a servant. Get so and so a drink...get that guy a sandwich...old country stuff' Worse!

'He used to yell at her and I think he hit her, too. Your father was glad she left him ... but he felt sorry for Augie.'

Augustine Martello, a toddler at the time, was left behind by Aunt Jo when she chose flight over fight.

'I figured since he was a boy,' she would say later on, 'that he'd have a better chance alone than Frances would.'

Augie was not alone long; Grandma took him in and he grew up at 81 Grand, living there when we had the apartment across the hall. Grandma was surrounded by family males. One memory of life at 81 Grand stands out.

It was early on a Saturday morning. Andrew and I were still in bed when Daddy came into the room, chuckling ...

'Look out the window,' he said. Joined by Daddy, the three of us lay across the width of the bed and looked onto the rainy corner of Elm and Grand. There in a drizzle was Mike backing up slowly and swinging an open umbrella back and forth to fend off three kids trying to get a whack at him.

Andrew said, 'Let's go ...'

But Daddy put a hand on his shoulder, 'No, wait ... I think he can take care of himself.' And sure enough, getting closer to the house, Mike darted into the back alley and in a couple of seconds was inside. We got to the kitchen as Mike kind of staggered through the door. A moment of silence, then we are all laughing.

Chapter 10
Contraband Stock

The State News which Daddy and Uncle Steve Fiato opened in 1948 at 132 State Street, in the shadow of the State Capitol, was a many-splendored thing (apologies for trivializing the great song, words by Paul Francis Webster, music by Sammy Fain and popularized by the Four Aces). In the heart of the State Street business district, it was eye-catching with its royal blue awning and neon signs. Daddy said the bettors were giving 2-1 that it wouldn't last six months. It far survived that and he and Steve cleaned up.

At one time or other, with the exception of Honey who was too young, we all worked at the State News, including Mother. At first, we were open 24 hours a day; that eventually shortened to 6 a.m.-midnight six days and all-night Saturday.

The Vigluccis didn't provide all the staff; the Fiatos equally participated, particularly Steve's son Joey, his brother Joe, and Aunt Nancy.

Mother didn't work there in the beginning and when she was about to make her State News debut, Daddy took me aside, gave me a pep talk about making Mother feel wanted, and added:

'Don't tell her about the rubbers.'

Though it was illegal, we sold Excello prophylactics. We kept them in the storage space of our Double-K nut machine. Our 'supplier' was some fly-by-night guy who used to come in selling from a suitcase full of goodies -- neckties, handkerchiefs, cuff-links, trinkets ... and rubbers. We sold a fair amount to regular customers who would rather deal with us regular guys than some nosy pharmacist. The price was right, too, three for 50 cents.

We sold just about everything. My cousin Joey Fiato, a fiery-faced redhead with a wild sense of humor, called the State News 'The Store of Three Wonders.'

A customer asked if we had a certain item. Joey looked for a while, found it, and remarked to the customer, 'That's why we call this the store of three wonders. You wonder if we got it, I wonder if we got it, and we both wonder how I found it.'

On another occasion, Johnny Dyke, one of the capital city's most successful and formidable track figures, asked Joey where he got the sunburn.

'In the sun,' the redhead shot back, leaving the redoubtable Dyke halfway between sputtering and chuckling.

The State News handled only class merchandise (with the possible exception of the Excellos). We had a wide supply of Yellow Bowl pipes; two humidor cases filled with a variety of cigars and pipe tobacco: the second largest display of pocketbooks (soft cover books) in Albany (only the famed Coulson's store on Broadway had more); Borden's 'Fit for a Golden Spoon' ice cream; newspapers from around the country; greeting cards; candy; soda; many more wonders than three.

We also sold souvenirs, notably bronze horses. Daddy and/or Steve would make the trip to a warehouse in New York City, buy a batch for later shipment. When they arrived, we would stick Albany, N.Y. decals on them and they would magically become souvenirs of the capital city.

Once I had to do the pricing on an arriving

case of souvenirs.

"Take the price on the invoice, double it and round it out to the next highest round figure,' was Daddy's instruction. Thus, if a tiny horse cost 35 cents, it would be doubled to 70 cents, then rounded out to $1.

Our largest brass horses sold for $17.95, a figure arrived at arbitrarily by Daddy who thought it sounded right.

A prime source of clientele for this merchandise, ironically, were tourists from New York City who considered us 'hicks.' They bought a lot of this stuff at prices twice what they would have paid back home. But then there would be no Albany, N.Y. decal. Still it was delightful having wiseacres from The City taking the horsies back where they came from.

Steve used to say, 'Guess who's the hick?' One time we had a batch of combs that wouldn't sell. They were 15 cents each and I said to Steve let's mark them down to a dime and get rid of them.

He chuckled and handed me a clear plastic container, 'Put them in this on the counter,' he said, 'write a little sign and stick it on the container, 'Get them while

they last -- 25 cents.' In a couple of days
they were gone.
But the variety inside the store was more
than matched by its clientele.

Chapter 11
A Place with Class

While the operators of the State News and their camp followers were anything but vanilla, it was the customers that gave the place panache. Case in point, Mark Devlin, a man probably in his early 60s, whose face told a story, make that an autobiography.

His spread nose said that he had been a fighter, probably a boxer and he was.

He was no longer in the best of shape, but he would at times break into a little shadow boxing.

'Still got it,' he'd say. Once or twice he would touch a big fist to my chin, 'KO!' he'd chuckle.

He would stop in the State News about 5:30 p.m. about an hour from his job as a guard at the Albany County Jail. It would be obvious to any Albanian that his position meant he had an in with the O'Connell family. He would change at the jail to bus it back to downtown. He was always in a suit and tie, well-dressed but no Beau Brummell, neither in fashion or personality. His shirt collar may at times be unbuttoned or turned up, and the 4-in-hand knot in his tie would be slid down some.

He would pick up the Knick News on the way to his Eagle Street apartment. I had the feeling he was a widower but he never talked about his wife--or women.

Basically, he was a loner and pleased to be so.

Different friends of mine might be hanging around the store when Mark would come in. He would stand by and not hide the fact that he was listening in on their conversation and though he might chuckle at a remark, or render a single clap of the hands in appreciation at some humorous anecdote or good news, he constrained himself from butting in.

I'd introduce him to whomever and he would grip their hand in that big powerful mitt of his.

One day, Robert Shryver, a CBA student, whom I met at the State News, spent a little time and when he left, Mark said.

'Got a lot of friends, don't you, kid ? Let me tell you something -- hang on to them because if you make it to my age, you'll be fortunate to have,' he stressed, 'one!'

I made a mental point of his 'if,' instead of 'when.'

Among those passing friends of his, according to Mark, were such acquaintances as Legs Diamond and Vincent 'Mad Dog' Coll, both of whom often visited State and Pearl.

Though his chatter was light, I noticed that from time to time, with only the two of us present, he would drop a golden nugget.

'Did you know, kid, that the O'Connells used to run a big gambling house in Florida?'

That stopped me in my tracks.

'Oh, sure and they stationed me there, as a guard.' He smiled thinly as he glanced about, making sure there were only four ears present.

'Easy job,' he said. 'Just stand in a corner and observe. Would you believe, a Tommy gun? Loaded, too. But we never had any trouble.'

The anecdote told me that at least one branch of the O'Connell operation was tinged with danger. It must have been my acne that allowed these guys to talk openly in front of me -- if they noticed me at all. Thus one day I overheard Johnny Dyke saying that someone, I didn't recognize the name, had borrowed an O'Connell automobile for the weekend and there was hell to pay when he returned it full of bullet holes.

Ironic it was that the crime-busting DA from Westchester County, Tom Dewey, occupied the gubernatorial seat in the state's widest open city. You'd think Albany's underside faced dark days but the rising Republican star simply stood aside and let gambling and other rackets steam on.

Another day, I was stunned at a State News conversation. Uncle Steve was telling my father about some overnight developments.

'They knocked off Willie, and Pete, and Doc, too.'

I butted in, 'They got killed?!'

'Mind your own business.' Daddy used his Jinx tone.

'But...' He could sense my stubborn curiosity was aroused.

'That doesn't mean anyone got killed, just

put out of business,' he explained.
We had a new governor, railroad-rich
Averill W. Harriman, up at the corner, and
such dire developments were not
expected at the hands of a Democrat.
Unbelievably, 'Honest Ave' let the word
out that the good old days were coming to
an end --he was cracking down on
gambling and other colorful Albany
activities.

Chapter 12
Central Casting

The State News, diversified that it was, chugged along. One chatty older lady came in Sunday mornings to pick up the paper. I was usually on duty but Mike also knew her. She was telling him of her theory that you can spot a person's honesty by the shape of his -- or her -- head. The more concave, the more trustworthy. And as an ancillary, homelier people could be trusted more. So, Mike said, 'What do you think of the guy who usually waits on you here?'

'Oh, he's one of the most honest people I know!' she exclaimed to Mike's delight.

Another of the State News cast of characters was a writer named Obie. He was kind of a gaunt guy, with a shock of straw-colored hair and a good-looking wife. They lived at the DeWitt Clinton Hotel at Eagle and State, a half-block from the store.

One Saturday night, Steve's brother Joey was on duty. This Joey was visually the opposite of red-haired cousin Joey. The older one was short and dark and, should we say, somewhat naive.

Obie got a bright idea -- at the unbright hour of 2 a.m. Joey didn't know Obie or his wife so Obie had her call him and invite him to meet her at a certain room near theirs in the hotel. They were kind enough to pick a room they knew was empty, then they looked on as Joey knocked on the door in vain and then finally left.

They waited a while and then Mrs. Obie called back asking Joey why he hadn't arrived. He explained why and sure enough in a few minutes was back at the door.

The third time, Joey declined the invitation.

Widely-known architect Harris (Harry) Sanders also got into the State News act. He had offices across State Street at the corner of Lodge, not far from a tailor whose sign read, 'Invisible Weaving.' Looking out his window one day, Harry spotted the other Joey Fiato, the red-haired teenager, step outside. Harry telephoned the store and when Joey answered, said in a stentorian voice, 'Joey, this is the Weaver speaking. Tend to business, stop hanging around outside.' Eventually, it got to the point where Harry would call three or four times every afternoon Joey was working.

'Who are you, Weaver?!' Joey would scream. 'Identify yourself. Where are you calling from, you coward!'

Across Lodge Street from the Invisible Weaver was an Albany landmark, St. Peter's Episcopal Church, which was easily visible from the State News. Judging from the number of people leaving Sunday services, St. Peter's always did all right. But on occasion, the throng would be larger and remain longer. Sure sign that the congregation that day included Thomas E. Dewey, the esteemed (elsewhere) governor of the State of New York.

Dewey was so unpopular with Albany denizens that they would boo him at opening day at Hawkins Stadium. This, even though, he was lenient with Albany gambling interests.

Hyman the Runner was a daily communicant at the newsroom. He was a disheveled, baldish guy, maybe 40. He made money by running bets around the network of houserooms and gambling spots. In a wrinkled sports jacket and mismatched slacks and open-collared shirt, he was constantly wiping his hand nervously over his head. His most distinguishing feature was some kind of metal cap in the front of his mouth, where a front tooth should have been. He was always poking at it with a toothpick.

He told anyone in sight that he had a serious claim of plagiarism. He said he wrote 'The Coffee Song' but it was stolen from him by Bob Hilliard and Richard Miles. To prove that he knew his way around a melody, he had another song he was trying to publish called 'Music in the Night.' He had it written on a crumpled piece of paper in his pocket which he zealously guarded.

'There's music in the night,
'And romance in the air ...
'My darling when you're near me,
'Love is everywhere.'
Then came the refrain:
'The night we met the moon above was shining,

*'But then somehow we lost the silver
lining,
'In dreams we meet again,
'To set our love aright,
'You once again are near me,
'And there's music in the night.'*

The cop on the beat was Al Gunderman, a
big, rosy-faced, bespectacled officer of the
old school. He gained some fame when he
ticketed Mayor Corning's official car
outside City Hall.

'I don't care,' he would say, 'whose car it
was. It was in a 'no parking' zone and that
was that.'

Al Gunderman's badge number was 112 --
which he played every day.

The Albany County district attorney was
Julian B. Erway, a quiet, unassuming,
distinguished and respected man who
would stand patiently in the numbers
lines at noontime, waiting to pay for his
newspaper.

A cabstand graced the curb outside and
the most colorful of the drivers was Ed
Marvin, from Montreal, Canada. A heavy-
set handsome man with short wavy dark
hair, Ed was always well-dressed and had
a 'tres formidable' air.

When he said he was formerly a cop in Montreal, we believed him. When he said he was a former chef, we believed him. We believed him because although there was something mysterious about him, he also had an offsetting amiable aura.

The people who ran the DeWitt Clinton Hotel at State and Eagle must have believed him, too, because he became the head chef there. And on Sundays when I worked the day shift, he often, very thoughtfully, would in person bring me a hot meal he prepared himself. Spaghetti! He should have known better -- it couldn't compare to Grandma's!

Ed Marvin was close to being the head of the State News class. Just a bit above him was Solly O'Connell, Uncle Dan's brother, known as the Big Guy, who fronted the family's gambling operations, among other things.

He always traveled with a retinue, including Johnny Dyke and other horse traders.

The State News sat in the midst of several downtown hotels -- the DeWitt Clinton favored by Democrats, a half-block away; the Wellington, next door; the Ten Eyck, for Republicans, just down the street on the opposite side. Tourist buses were coming and going, so sometimes on a Sunday afternoon we would get extremely busy.

One such Sunday we were besieged by thirsty customers, raiding our bright red, cold water Coca Cola cooler in the back part of the store. I gave up trying to store the empties in their racks to wait on New York City tourists buying souvenir brass horses. Then Solly and his cortege stopped in. The Big Guy went to the cooler and began making obvious noises of discomfort, pretending it was impossible to get a soda out because of the empties left on the lid.

Finally, when he saw that his sounds were not getting proper attention, he said, 'Hey, kid, you should keep the place neater than this.'

'There's a rag back there if you want it,' I wished I said. Solly waved his minions out as he left, saying, 'We'll be back when it's not so busy.'

I only relate this story because I never think of myself as such a wise guy, especially at 16. It wasn't bright to be a smart alec with Solly for obvious reasons, but even more so because he was a good customer.

The O'Connells used to put on cockfights at their home in the Helderbergs, just south of Albany, lasting over the weekend. On Friday nights, the usual group would stop at the State News and buy out the Double K nuts, Borden's Fit for a Golden Spoon ice cream, lots of cigarettes and Dyke cigars, and, yes, soda of all varieties. Maybe a hundred dollar's worth. So it was not good business to be a wisenheimer with that crowd.

At the time, Carmine DeSapio was head man of the Tammany Hall machine in New York City. I have no information that he ever attended the cockfight but on one occasion he and Dan O'Connell were having a cocktail, or maybe a State News soda, when O'Connell opened the draperies over a huge picture window. In the distance were the bright lights of the City of Albany. O'Connell said to his political associate, 'Behold, the Holy City!'

Chapter 13
Farewell, Mark Devlin

Jack Devine seemed a cut above the many denizens of Albany's gambling world. I think he was in a higher echelon of the O'Connell machine. I can still see him now -- a slim man, fiftyish, in a well-tailored camel-hair overcoat, button-down shirt and rep tie -- natty, with an aura of intelligence.

Jack managed the horse room over Coulson's newstand on Broadway. Coulson's was no mere front for a horse room; it had a thriving business which was envied by the operators of the State News up State Street near the Capitol. Coulson's had the largest selection of paperbacks in Albany, newspapers from all over, plus all the usual sundries of a newsroom. But walk straight through to the back, through a door, up the stairs and there you were in reputedly the biggest horse room in town.

There was the usual tote board with the odds of the races being called that day, a guy with a pole eraser changing the odds as they shifted. A radio would be blaring actual calls of races as they were run and a teller behind a cage took bets on any race anywhere still to be run that day.

Saturday, for obvious reasons, was always a big day. When I was about 16, Bob Sweeney and I used to stop there once in a while. On one such occasion, Jack Devine called me to the teller's cage and handed me an envelope with Mark Devlin's name on it.

'Here, kid,' he said, 'take this to Mark at St. Peter's.'

I knew Mark was in the hospital. Someone had found him one cold night huddled in his camel-haired coat in the basement entrance of his apartment on Eagle Street, not far from the Governor's Mansion. He had pneumonia.

'Here's a fin,' Devine continued, 'take a cab there. Don't open the envelope, cabeesh?'

I don't know if Jack was trying to impress me with his linguistic skills or if he thought Italians loved people to try their language.

'Okay,' I said, the five-dollar bill quickly finding a new home in my pocket; naturally I took the New Scotland Avenue bus for 15 cents.

I found out Mark's room number and, looking in thought somebody made a mistake. There was this thin, emaciated, elderly man in the bed. I snapped outside and leaned against a wall. Slowly I realized that it was indeed Mark who, the last time I saw him, was an energetic guy almost shadow-boxing up State Street.

For a quick moment, I thought I'd hand the note to a nurse but that wouldn't be right. I took a breath and went back into his room.

'Hi, Mark,' I said too loudly and too brightly.

His eyes opened and with a faint smile, he said, 'Hey, kid, how are you?' For the first time, I realized he had false teeth. His flattened nose seemed more grotesque in his cheekless face. His thin gray hair was pasted back by sweat.

'Geez, what are you doing here?'

'Just came to see you,' I lied … 'and Jack Devine said to give you this.' I thrust the envelope at him.

He took it, reached for his horn-rimmed glasses and even with them on squinted at the large lettering 'MARK DEVLIN' on the outside. He tore it open, took some time to read the contents and when the message sank in started chuckling.

'Didn't I tell you,' he began, using that Albany way of making a question of a statement, 'that they'd take care of me? Didn't I?' Actually he had, but in a different context. He handed the letter to me – 'Read it.'

Scrawled in big letters was the message: 'Mark, don't pay for nothing. The Big Guy will take care of everything.'

No 'Hope you're feeling well'; no 'Get well soon.' And it was unsigned -- Albany style. It may have seemed cold to me but to Mark it was Florida all over again. His attitude immediately changed. He shifted his body so he could sit up. "You wouldn't want something to eat, would you?" I looked around the room; there was nothing there -- no candy, no flowers, no cards.

'I mean I'll ring for something,' he chuckled. 'It'll be taken care of' -- he was making quick use of his new-found largesse. I demurred.

'Did I tell you that they gave me that camel-hair coat? The nurses said if it weren't for that coat, I would have died right there in the doorway. Good people, kid.'

I wondered why I didn't exactly agree and awkwardly began to make my exit.

'Any message for me to take back, Mark?'

'Nah,' he jauntily waved off any encumbrances. 'Just tell Jack I'm fine and that I said thanks to Solly.'

I turned back one more time as I was leaving his room. He had already begun to read the note again, as if studying some sort of legal document, which, after all, I guess it was. I hesitated in the doorway, then left.

It was the last time I ever saw Mark.

Chapter 14
Career Opportunity

Johnny Dyke, who ran one of the best horserooms in Albany, frequented the State News and Willie Gordon and even Sollie O'Connell came in often but Jack Devine rarely did. So when he offered me a job at the horse room I figured someone else must have touted me.

'All day Saturday -- every Saturday,' he said. '$35.'

'But what could I do?' I asked.

'Mostly work the tote board ... other things ... errands.'

He could see by my expression that I was hesitant. 'Think it over ... talk to Jinx.'

That was exactly what I did. I put it off for a couple of days then one day at the State News, I asked Daddy about it.

'Nah,' he said, 'every Saturday -- you're already working the midnight shift here. But it's up to you. It's not the right thing to do -- but it's your decision. "And if you do it, don't tell your mother.'

Who said I never listened to my father. I decided against it -- and I never told Jack

Devine -- in fact, I never went to the horse room again.

Dyke owned a cigar factory. I don't know how or why or where. One rumor had it that he won it gambling. But Daddy and Steve made a deal with him when they opened the State News. I recall Daddy saying they got $600, or the neon sign cost $600 and Johnny Dyke paid for it.

The sign read State News and below it in script Dyke Cigars.

We kept Johnny's cigars in two cylindrical containers on top of the counter, as well as in the humidors. They cost 20 cents each, which was a good price for a stogie in those days.

Johnny was a dapper dresser -- dark blue camel-hair overcoat, grey fedora, white shirt, dark tie. Always the cigar. His horse room backed our bets. It was up State Street; I never went there. The way it worked: people would place bets in our store and we had a 50-50 deal with Dyke. We kept 50 percent of the take but we also were responsible for paying 50 percent of our customer's winnings. Johnny played the same number every day -- 486, $5 straight. If it hit, he would get $2,400 (the actually payoff was $3,000 but the State News would get 20 percent or $600. In addition, we kept 10 percent of all the take on numbers).

'Bring it in,' he would say when he played the number 'and it'll be biscuit city for you, too.'

He seldom came close. The numbers would be released one at a time from the race track -- Narragansett was used in fair weather. Anyone could figure out the number -- add the parimutuels for the first three races, third digit from the left, something like that, would be the first number, and so forth for the next two. Our backer would call in the first number about 1:30, the second around 3:30 and the final number about 5.

Because the numbers were illegal we did not put them in the window; that could be provocative. Instead we put them up one at a time on the side of the telephone booth, which could be seen through the window.

One day the first two numbers were 4 and 8. It didn't take Johnny very long to call. 'Bring in the 6,' he rasped over the telephone. 'And you've got a c-note.'

Well, it didn't work out. I can't remember the last number but it wasn't a 6.

'Gonna play something different?' I asked Johnny the next day. 'You crazy?' he snapped. 'What if 486 comes out?' That was a chance no gambler could take.

People made money lots of ways from the numbers, the most democratic gambling game ever devised --a person could bet a penny. Somebody might bet a nickel -- one cent straight on five different numbers. If one of them came out the payoff would be $5.40.

You could also play the number boxed -- then if the three numbers came out in some different order, you would get $27 per dollar.

Number dream books were published. If you dreamed about a can of spinach, or Popeye, look it up, it would tell what number you should play.

The most popular number was 132, the baby gig. But at times it would be outplayed by some number, say, popping up in the news.

Babe Ruth died at 8:15 August 16, 1948. The next day almost everybody played 815 -- well, maybe not Johnny Dyke -- and it hit! It was the first time in history, they said, the backers weren't able to pay off the same day. The bettors had to wait until the next day to collect their winnings.

Babe Ruth ... an American hero!

Democracy in Action

You also could play the numbers at Sadie Burns' corner store on Van Woert Street. No one thought it odd for Sadie and her older sister Lizzie, both proper spinsters in their late 60s or 70s, to be writing numbers.

And you could bet farther down Van Woert, at Mellie Wolfgang's house. Just go around to the back porch, knock on the door and Mellie or Mrs. Wolfgang would take your bet. My Grandmother Delia used to send me there and once in a while Bernard Milos and I would bet, pretending someone in our family sent us.

Mrs. Wolfgang was an outgoing sort but her husband was quiet. He had been a pitcher for the ill-famed Chicago Black Sox, though not involved in the scandalous part. He never talked about it. It was strange to think that with baseball all around him, including the Tigers with their clubhouse right up the street, Mellie, teammate of Shoeless Joe Jackson himself, never took part. He kept to himself, this former major leaguer in our baseball-crazy midst.

Chapter 15
1939 'The Greatest Year'

Bernard Milos was the first kid my age I met when we moved to Van Woert Street from Grand Street in the summer of 1938. His father, also Bernard, worked at the C. T. Hubbell lumber yard at Broadway and Tivoli. Mr. Milos was very quiet, maybe somber, but actually was not an unfriendly man. Bernard's mother, Bertha, was gregarious with a twinkle in her eye which made her attractive. On Van Woert we honored all adults as Mr. or Mrs. But I think if we were to have gotten on a first name basis with any it would have been Mrs. Milos, she was that accessible. Bernard and I were six when we first met in the vacant lot next to Pop's house at 98 Van Woert Street. For the next several years he was my best friend, confidante, and fellow traveler. After the ninth grade at Philip Livingston we went separate ways -- I to Albany High and Bernard to Christian Brothers Academy ... never has a twain been farther apart. When our family moved to Clinton Avenue in 1948, we never saw each other again. Decades later, my cousin Joan Waters told me Bernard Milos died young -- 'bad heart, I think.'

I believe the Milos family was Lithuanian but because there were so many Poles on the street, we just lumped them in and called them Polish, too.

Neighborhood kids didn't spend much time in each other's houses, but I was in Bernard's more than any other.

And when seeking each other out we didn't knock on doors or ring bells. We merely stood outside, preferably in the backyard, and actually sang the person's name --- 'Hey, Ber-nard!' The name had to be at least two syllables for the proper meter.

Bernard and I went to St. Joseph's Academy together, had connecting paper routes, played together on Jigger Hayes' Tiger baseball team, chased after Patsy Kelly and Joan Shipley from St. Joseph's as early as the third grade, went to movies both downtown and at the Paramount on Clinton Avenue, attended Albany Senators games at Hawkins Stadium in Menands, and went to high school basketball games all over town.

Mostly we played around Van Woert Street, developing muscular imaginations. We never agreed on anything. I liked Bing Crosby, he Sinatra; I favored Sealtest (my uncle Mickey was a milkman there), RC Cola, the American League, Joe DiMaggio, Gene Autry; Bernard preferred Borden's, Pepsi, the National League, Ted Williams, Roy Rogers. Name it, he took the other side. Nationality or religion was never at the basis of our disagreement; such as Italian or Lithuanian ' oops! Such could not be said for others in this short tome. Think of the Italian classic singers Caruso, Gigli, Lanza, Martinelli or, in later years, Pavarotti.

'That's all right,' Pops might say, 'John McCormack was the equal of all of them,-- Together,' Pops believed.

And he also accepted Ella Fitzgerald as a second cousin.

We had tacit agreements. One sweltering summer day in 1939, when we were seven, we spent an afternoon traipsing through the heavy weeds in the field between my backyard and the Colonie Street dumps. We called the area

Hispaniola. That summer we were fascinated by the carcass of a dead dog out in the weeded fields and we went to check on the rot ever day, inspecting it to see if there were more or less maggots than the day before.

We used sticks to slash at the tall weeds in our way, being careful of the silky webs which were home to giant yellow jackets and other spiders. One particularly ugly species had a bulbous pink, bloated body.

'I'll bet that's a poisonous one,' I said.

'Nah, it's not,' Bernard countered.

After a while, we would make our way to the top of the dump, gathering the lids off the squat coffee cans of the period which included twist keys to cut the tops off. The lids made for great scaling, ala the futuristic Frisbees.

We stood at the top of the dump, flinging the lids.

"The air is perfect today,' Bernard said.

'Yesterday was better,' I replied.

We would go down and retrieve the lids, being careful not to disrupt any rats.

'Rats aren't so bad,' Mr. Milos told us once. 'But if they think you're after them, watch out! I cornered one in my cellar and he jumped right through the air at my throat.'

'That must have really scared your father,' I said later.

'Nah, he made it up,' Bernard said.

We spotted Mrs. Bick's cow grazing in Hispaniola, behind the houses on Van Woert. For some reason, Bernard's lids kept going in that direction.

'Don't throw at the cow,' I said.

'I'm not, the wind is taking them,' he protested.

On the way back down, we found a rusty iron rod, jammed it through two coffee cans making slots for the sticks. We inserted them, thus making swords, our hands protected by the erstwhile coffee tins. We worked up a sweat slashing and parrying, Errol Flynn vs. Tyrone Power, on top of the little hill halfway between my backyard and the dump.

After a while, we went to my yard, near our homemade clubhouse.

Bernard stopped in the weeds to relieve himself; a pensive expression on his seven-year-old face.

"You know,' he said, '1939 is really the best year ever.'

We Called Them Movies

FYI: Produced that year were 'Gone with
the Wind,' 'The Wizard of Oz,' 'Beau Geste,'
(Gary Cooper, Ray Milland); 'Each Dawn I
Die,' 'Drums Along the Mohawk,'
'Gulliver's Travels,' 'Destry Rides Again,'
(Marlene Dietrich, James Stewart); 'Dust
Be My Destiny,'(we all worshiped John
Garfeld); 'Gunga Din,'(Cary Grant, Douglas
Fairbanks Jr., Victor McGlaglen, Joan
Fontaine); 'Jesse James,' (Tyrone Power
and Henry Fonda); 'Juarez,' with the great
star Paul Muni; 'Ninotchka,' (Greta Garbo),
'Northwest Passage'; 'Nurse Edith Cavell';
'The Roaring Twenties,' (James Cagney,
Humphrey Bogart, Jeffrey Lynn);
'Goodbye Mr. Chips'; 'Stagecoach.'
Irving Berlin wrote a song called 'God
Bless America,' performed by the songbird
of Dixie, Kate Smith; West Coast writer
John Steinbeck published 'The Grapes of
Wrath'; 'Life with Father' was on
Broadway, and Coleman Hawkins
recorded the saxophone masterpiece
'Body and Soul.'
But our idyllic life was nontheless

shattered -- evil seeped even unto Van Woert Street. In September, a man we had never heard of ' Adolph Hitler ' led his gang of monster bullies in the invasion of Poland. This was especially troublesome because of the high percentage of Van Woert Street Poles (all right, Lithuanians) and it also brought us into history's greatest conflict.

In another sphere that year, on July 4, the Iron Horse of baseball, Lou Gehrig, revealed he was 'domitable,' announcing his retirement from 'the game' because of something called -' amyotrophic lateral sclerosis.

Was Ma Already
In a Parallel World?

As I remember it, the Strand on North Pearl Street played first-run Warner Brothers movies. In retrospect, it seems impossible to believe, but I remember Ma took me there a few times. We saw "Each Dawn I Die,' 'The Roaring Twenties' and 'Nurse Edith Cavell' there.

Maybe my mother also went with us, but I

just don't remember it that way. Ma was practically an invalid so we couldn't have walked; we didn't own a car, and the exigencies of taking a bus would have been insurmountable.

Memories are tricky. ' I know I saw those movies with Ma -- though it just plain would be impossible. Unless Ma was the true 'Queen of the Silver Screen.' In a parallel existence. It could be possible ... We are half Irish, you know!

Chapter 16
World Travelers

After Bernard had made his urinary respects to the greatest movie year, we went to Sadie's. We had some money we had collected by returning empty bottles (2 cents each) and from selling some stuff to Joe Phelan at his junkyard next to The Diamond. We splurged. The usual: two devil's food cakes; two sodas (one RC, one Pepsi), and the rest on penny candy, maybe even the 2-cent Grade A chocolate blocks.

As we often did, we went up to Goat Mountain, halfway up the Swan Street hill, on the left, next to the shortcut to Ten Broeck Street. From Goat Mountain (Pop and his peers, two generations earlier, more conservatively and accurately called it Goat Hill) we could survey a good part of the area terrain while we indelicately enjoyed the nutritious cake, soda and candy lunch.

You may have noticed we never washed our hands. We should have, you say? TS! So you'll know, TS was a popular phrase;

mostly it was more acceptable than 'tough titties.' And it more accurately stood for 'tough situation,' or, heaven forbid, 'tough shit.' Bernard and I never felt confined to Van Woert Street and traveled far and wide long before we reached double digits in age. One of our favorite spots was where the stream carrying outlet sewage from West Albany tumbled over a falls to rush under Broadway headed for the mighty Hudson. It was known as 'Shit Creek.'

In cooler weather, it wasn't so bad but in July it was odoriferous. This particular day, we hung around until the thrill wore off and we headed down to the river.

In about five minutes, we were on the flats alongside the Mighty Hudson. When the tide was in all the way from the Atlantic, the center of the river loomed higher than the shores. Rensselaer was on the other side where the residents actually used filtered Hudson River water for drinking. A popular sign in Albany public restrooms read: Please flush toilets; Rensselaer needs water.'

Mother didn't like me (make that hated) going down to the river; she was deathly afraid of any body of water larger than our kitchen sink. Daddy didn't share that fear of water, he just didn't like to drink it. The point is though that on occasions we spent time at the river, I kept it a family secret.

Willie Haupt, aka Hoptoad, sometimes shortened to Hop, often accompanied us to the river.

We all kind of thought of Hop as, I guess, dumb. Granted . Or were we the slow ones? He lived with his grandfather across Van Woert Street from the Tiger AC. They looked and dressed how we pictured farmers. Mr. Haupt often used rustic expressions: 'The ground is as dry as toe punk,' was our favorite.

Willie was on the tall side, with a long, oval face, pale blue eyes, and he wore coveralls. His yellow hair lay flat on his head. He didn't often pal around with the rest of us; he just didn't fit in (or maybe we didn't). I don't ever remember him playing ball or even being at The Diamond.

The three of us, however, would rent a rowboat every so often (I think a dollar an hour) and paddle around on the Hudson.

Those two would strip down to their skivvies and dive in to swim. One day, a dead cow floating by almost took Hop under. Because I couldn't swim I only went in once or twice and just hung onto the side of the boat.

Mostly, we would drift along and listen to Hoptoad sing. His favorite was Burl Ives, someone Bernard and I hadn't heard of before. We preferred the Mills Brothers (Bernard) or the Ink Spots (me).

'I love my rooster, my rooster loves me,' Hop would sing. 'I love my rooster by the cottonwood tree, I love my rooster, my rooster loves me, cockle dee doodle, dee doodle dee dee.'

He could sing 'Bluetail Fly' and 'Jimmy Cracked Corn,' all the way through. Another in his repertoire was 'Paper Doll,' a Mills Brothers hit. With all that schtick, he couldn't be dumb. But the legend persisted.

Well, there was something down by the riverside that would have surprised all our parents if we told them. In two or three ramshackle shacks, lived some 'Jakie Bums.' We got to know one -- Louie. I avoided him but Willie and Bernard eventually found him friendly. They would visit Louie the Bum in his humble abode. I was able to resist the honor.

One of the last times I saw Willie Haupt, the three of us ' Bernard, Willie and I -- were 'eeling' in the Hudson at twilight, an eerie and quiet time on the river. We used hand-reels, flinging the line out from the shore. When you caught an eel, you didn't reel it in, you swung it as high in the air as possible and tried to bash it on the ledges behind us to kill it before it snarled up the line all to hell. Then we would throw the slippery creatures back into the river.

'Like snakes,' Hop said. 'Can you imagine, some people eat those things?'

'Only crazy people,' Bernard said.

I didn't tell them that Grandma considered them a delicacy.

I can't remember ever seeing Willie Haupt after that summer. The last I heard about him, someone said he was off to the Korean War.

The FBI and Aunt Kate

In our house at 98 Van Woert Street, the refrigerator stood between the kitchen door and a window opening to the backyard. At some time it must have replaced the icebox because I can remember both. However, though the change must have been a gala occasion, I can't recall it.

Our young Aunt Catherine lived with us for some time during World War II. She was fun indeed and the house was rich with laughter having her there. Consider that it was home to its owner Pop, and my father Jinx, who had a busy life outside it, my mother, Catherine, two children, Honey and I, and was the former abode of my grandmother who died in 1940, as well as brothers Mike and Andrew who at the time of this incident were both in the Navy (U.S., that is).

Catherine was also known as Kate, which probably better matched her ebullient personality. When this happened, she was between husbands. Jerry Metzger, her first mate, was nice to us kids but apparently less so with Catherine. They lived on First Street on Arbor Hill and I forever endeared myself to Catherine when I stayed with her overnight once at that abode -- I was the first of all my generation to so 'honor' my youngest aunt.

Single and in her 20s, Catherine had a great job -- operator at the telephone company. One day she met tall, dark and handsome Frank Cardamone who lived on Colonie Street, also of Arbor Hill society. I didn't know it at the time, but he was the same-name uncle of Frankie Cardamone, who was to be my school friend and baseball teammate.

Apparently, Catherine, who was the tallest of the Fitzgerald sisters, and attractive, and Frank hit it off quickly. Catherine, at least, was interested in a long-term relationship, judging by her first question: 'What do you do"

'FBI,' Frank smiled broadly.

'The FBI?'

'Sure,' the smile persisted.

'Gee, the Federal Bureau of Investigation?'

'Oh, no,' The smile remained, 'A different FBI.'

'Oh?' Catherine was confused.

'Full-blooded Italian,' the snappy nod of his head affirmed his station in life.

Though it was fleeting, it wasn't the first mention of the FBI in Catherine's life. One summer day, a knock at the back screen door revealed two men dressed in business clothes standing on the step. Catherine, ever sensitive to bill collectors, quickly slid into one of her favorite positions, crouching alongside the refrigerator blocking sight of her from the door.

I was sitting, drawing, at the table at the window on the right side of the kitchen. Mother said hello to the men, not exactly welcoming them, but quickly went out, talking to them a short time in the backyard.

When the men left, Catherine asked Mother, 'Who were they?'

She was aghast when Mother answered calmly, 'The FBI.'

'The FBI?' Catherine exclaimed. 'What did they want with you?'

'Not me ... they wanted to talk to Jinx.'

'About what?' Catherine and I were both eager for answers.

'Nothing important,' Mother said and over the years she was adamant about refusing to describe the conversation. To me, it was either 'none of my business' or 'nothing important.'

As far as I know, the FBI agents never returned; if they did, Mother was mum about it.

Chapter 17
Another Visit

Would you believe that about the same time, in fact, March 12, 1942, a scarily similar meeting was taking place in Mamaroneck, N.Y. In this scenario, the woman, Doris Pinza, an American of English descent, was grocery shopping and her Italian immigrant husband was alone doing paperwork in an upstairs room of their home when he suddenly became aware of the presence of two strange men.

The pair had entered through an unlocked back door without knocking or using the doorbell and had moved quietly up the stairs.

One of them said, 'Are you Ezio Pinza?'

'Yes.' The startled Italian with the rugged visage stood slowly.

'What can I do for you?'

The men showed their FBI credentials and one said, 'In the name of the President of the United States, we place you under arrest.'

The major star of the Metropolitan Opera was shocked and puzzled and handcuffed.

'Could you wait until my wife comes

home?'

'Sure, we intend to search your home anyway.'

They did just that and found nothing. Pinza's wife, Doris, recounts that the Justice Department wouldn't disclose the charges.

'When they had finished their search of every room, closet, drawer and file and found nothing of interest except a bill of sale for our boat, they told us they were going to take Ezio to the Foley Square Court House in Manhattan. When they arrived there, Ezio was searched again, fingerprinted, and questioned at length. He was then taken by boat to Ellis Island and handed over to uniformed guards who took away his necktie, belt and shoelaces. Finally, Ezio was assigned an upper cot in a huge dormitory.'

And they were not allowed to bring a lawyer into the courtroom.

I had utter confidence in my husband,' Doris said, 'and although I was confused, I felt certain that some horrible mistake had been made and that he would be released quickly. But I was soon told that he could not be released until after a hearing that would take place in 12 days time -- that was chilling news.

'We were told that the United States Department of Justice would not disclose to us what charges had been brought against Ezio. Needless to say, that seemed to us a highly unusual and unfair policy for an American court.

'Ezio was totally innocent of any wrongdoing against the country,' his wife continued. 'He was due to receive his citizenship papers in four months and we had not the slightest idea of what allegations had been made. How, we agonized, could we prepare for a hearing in 12 days? What would we talk about? What allegations did we have to rebut?'

Doris was allowed to visit her husband for about 15 minutes once a week and had to go through a humiliating body search each time.

Still, though the Pinzas had faith in American justice, he was not cleared. Newspapers finally focused on the event, reporting he had been arrested as an 'enemy alien' and that he might be guilty of subversive activities.

'Ezio and I were forced to face a stern

panel without legal assistance and without knowledge of the charges,' Doris said. 'We did our best to defend ourselves against the ghosts lined up against us. Not surprisingly, we failed.'

'Two judges voted for acquittal and one did not,' she said. 'We were told that Ezio would be shipped to a camp in some distant state until the end of the war. He would never be allowed to have any visitors, and I could send him only one letter a month.'

Their situation was bleak but, fortunately, the Pinzas did have some clout and were granted a second hearing. Colleagues began to step forward to defend him and testify under oath about how the drama had been invented and about the impossibility of his being any type of threat to America. The world-famous author Thomas Mann wrote a letter in his support. The famed New York City anti-fascist leader Carlo Tresca declared, 'Ezio Pinza has never shown himself to be directly or indirectly, an agent of fascism or Mussolini.'

'This time we succeeded,' Doris said. On July 2, 1945, Ezio was honored to be chosen to sing the national anthem at the welcoming home ceremony for Generals George Patton and Jimmy Doolittle. Pinza's granddaughter Sarah Goodyear wrote in a Village Voice article, 'When Being Italian Was a Crime,' that her grandfather's offense 'was being an Italian national in a country that had just declared war against Japan, Germany and Italy. People who did not like him were whispering about his sympathy for his native land. That was enough for J. Edgar Hoover.

'My grandfather was a famous man,' Goodyear wrote, 'the leading basso at the Metropolitan Opera and his arrest was reported prominently in the national press. He became Hoover's trophy.

'Other Italians in America didn't have such important friends. A few spent months and even years in internment camps in places as isolated as Montana. On the west coast, Italian nationals were forbidden to enter neighborhoods or entire towns that were deemed to be of military importance. And some of them lost their jobs and their homes. Some 10,000 people were displaced ... another 50,000 lived under curfew.'

All of that, and his 850 appearances at the Metropolitan Opera became only of background interest for the ultimate Ezio Pinza story. Six short years later, in 1948, the musical world was stunned when Pinza left the Met to become Emil DeBeque, the self-exiled Frenchman in the legendary musical 'South Pacific.' Who will forget arguably the most romantic song ever when the trim 55-year-old rendered 'Some Enchanted Evening,' ranging from basso profundo to falsetto. It could have been another dishonor to be chalked up against the sinister J. Edgar Hoover -- depriving the world of the Rodgers and Hammerstein masterpiece. And though the Pinzas weathered the tempest in 1942, they nonetheless were stricken by the stress. This was evidenced by the fact that they never discussed the situation as a family. Doris didn't tell her own daughter until years later, then only briefly.

'We put it out of our minds and behind us,' Doris explained. 'I didn't tell any of the children until they were grown. We were so ashamed.'

Sarah Goodyear's mother, Clelia Garrity, who was Ezio's daughter, said her father never talked about the matter with her or her younger brother and sister.

'That silence is typical in families where loyalty to America was questioned,' said Joseph Scelsa, dean of the Italian-American Institute at Queens College. 'It's a cultural legacy ... of taking it on the chin, of being quiet about it.'

We Americans seem to have a tradition of distrusting new Americans. We saw it with Ezio Pinza. We saw it earlier when Sacco and Vanzetti were executed for a crime they didn't commit as the government acted out of fright and ignored the Constitution.

Yes, the Italians experienced it. So did the Irish; witness the employment signs of the early 20th century -- 'Irish Need Not Apply.'

And when they weren't defending themselves against such injustice, the Italians and Irish took the time to belittle each other. It's the All-American way.

Enrico Fermi
The Italian Navigator

One of our favorites in those radio days
was 'I Love a Mystery.'
Well, do YOU love a mystery? And are you
further fascinated when a mystery is
wrapped around a life-and-death scenario
of world significance? Hang on.
December 2, 1942, dawned in frigid
below-zero temperatures in Chicago. The
country was in the midst of World War II
and that morning the State Department
announced that two million Jews had
perished in Europe and that Americans
and Japanese were engaged in ferocious
fighting on Guadalcanal Island in the
Pacific.
At that time, while we were shivering in
Sister Domenica's fifth grade, a group of
middle-aged men in overcoats were
gathered on a balcony over the cold
squash court beneath the University of
Chicago football stadium.
Most eyes were fastened on a dark,
compact man with mischievous blue-grey
eyes working in a wood-framed structure
he called in his foreign accent a 'pile.' As

he manipulated the equipment, and a certain reaction transpired, he allowed himself a slow grin.

History had been made.

The group assembled included among the top international scientific minds of the era. They had just witnessed the first chain reaction in uranium, the initial step toward nuclear fission and the atomic bomb.

The U.S. administration official on hand had to use code to send this staggeringly momentous report via telephone to Washington. 'The Italian navigator,' he said, 'has landed in the new world.'

This modern-day Columbus was a 41-year-old Italian physicist named Enrico Fermi. And his accomplishment might well rival that of Columbus in the history of the world.

Fermi had come a long way from his birth in Rome, the son of a civil servant, Alberto Fermi, and his wife Ida de Gattis.

At a very young age, Enrico was shattered by the death of his beloved brother Giulio during minor throat surgery.

Poor but extremely gifted in mathematics and physics, Enrico couldn't afford new books, so he often browsed through the used-book stalls at the famous Campo de Fiori in Rome.

Ironically, he probably passed beneath the statue of Giordano Bruno who was tortured and burned by the papal inquisition on that very spot. It is not very clear exactly why he was executed though among many other ideas he professed that the universe was infinite. Whether his crucial differences with the Church were of an astronomical nature or religious, he stuck by what he saw as the truth even unto death.

Following his brother's death, the grief-stricken teen came across two antique volumes of elementary physics, carried them home, and read them through, sometimes correcting the math. Later, he told his sister Maria that he was so fascinated he hadn't even noticed the tomes were written in Latin.

He was indeed a genius.

His competition essay to university was judged worthy of a doctoral thesis. By 1920, when he was 19, Fermi, always supremely self-assured, was instructing his teachers at the University of Pisa.

At 25, he was a full professor in theoretical physics in his hometown of Rome. He assembled a small group of first-class, talented young scientists and took on the task of reviving Italian physics. His followers, judging him infallible, dubbed him 'The Pope.'

Now comes another dramatic, frightening and crucial development in the life of Enrico Fermi and the entire world. This 'pope' and his Italian team almost discovered nuclear fission in 1934 in the course of experiments in which, looking for radioactive transformations, they systematically bombarded one element after another with the newly discovered neutron.

They missed founding nuclear fission by the thickness of the sheet of foil in which they wrapped their uranium sample and which blocked the fission fragments that their instruments would otherwise have recorded.

This well could also have created the trite figure of speech 'a blessing in disguise.' If the fission had come to light in Rome in the mid-1930s, while the democracies still slept (apologies to JFK), Fascist Italy and

Nazi Germany would have won a long lead toward development of the atomic bomb. The course of history ... well not let's not even think of that.

As it was, Fermi, whose wife Laura Capon was Jewish, escaped Fascist persecution and left for America, where he landed in 1938 with a Nobel Prize he had won for his work on cosmic rays.

His near-miss on nuclear fission in 1934 was not without gain. He made the most important discovery of his life -- that slowing neutrons by passing them through a light-element moderator such as paraffin increased their effectiveness, a finding that would allow releasing nuclear energy in a reactor. Thus he was on his way to inventing the nuclear reactor and his Chicago experiment.

One of Fermi's racial predecessors, Leonardo da Vinci, once said knowledge was easy, all one had to do was 'see.' Look at the life and the things around you, study them and you will learn. Simple. Fermi understood the importance of such simplicity. He was on hand at Los Alamos in the New Mexico desert for the first atomic bomb explosion in July 1945. How did he measure the explosiveness? In the pre-dawn stillness before the explosion, he dropped fragments of paper and repeated this when the blast's wind arrived. He gauged the effect by measuring the displacement between the two groups of fragments.

Though Fermi was dubbed in some circles as the Father of the Atomic Bomb, he was not disposed to using nuclear weapons. He argued against U.S. development of the hydrogen bomb in 1949, calling it 'a weapon which in practical effect is almost one of genocide.'

He was not heeded.

Fermi became an American citizen in 1944. He and his wife Laura had two children, Giulio and Nella. His favorite pastimes were walking, mountaineering, and winter sports. He died of stomach cancer at the young age of 53.

A debt of gratitude to Pulitzer Prize winner Richard Rhodes, author of 'The Making of the Atomic Bomb.'

Chapter 18
Clark Gable's Dilemma

We spent a lot of time looking for baseballs we'd hit into the weeds, or off the field, at The Diamond. One day, in the lot just to the east toward the river, next to Joe Phelan's junkyard, a bunch of us were looking through the weeds and the curbstones the city had dumped there. 'Rimrock Canyon,' cousin Jack Regan had named the lot, I think after some B Western.

Tommy Delaney was expounding on the value of a single penny. He was built kind of square and walked like a lefthander. He had a largish, also squarish head, with a shock of brown hair, big, brown eyes.

'Clark Gable,' according to Delaney, his wide-hinged jaw flapping Joe E. Brown style, 'wanted to buy the rights to *Gone with the Wind.* They wanted a million dollars.'

Now he had all of our attention; we stopped scouring the ground.

'Clark (suddenly first-name basis) went around to everybody and he had a lot of money himself. After scraping and begging everything he could, he wound up with nine hundred and ninety-nine thousand, nine hundred and ninety-nine dollars, and ninety-nine cents,' Tommy said. 'He couldn't come up with one more penny and he lost the deal.'

We all just stood there amidst the chicory soaking in this predicament. Finally, Bernard asked, 'Where did you hear about this?'

'I read it ... in a movie magazine at Rocco's.'

Rocco DiDonna owned a barbershop on Swan Street next to Mike's Log Cabin which advertised, 'If you must drive your husband to drink, drive him to Mike's Log Cabin.'

We were all silent trying to ingest Delaney's story.

Finally -- 'You're full of shit,' the ever-astute Bernard noted.

'Well, it's better than just looking for the ball,' Tommy said laughing, his mouth gaping to his ears.

Chapter 19
Boys and Girls Together

Lest anyone should think Van Woert Street was strictly Boys Town, Elaine Rhatigan (a clear-skinned, early-teen beauty with longish dark hair) should be mentioned. And her sister Sissy (maybe curlier hair), and her sister Betty (curlier and almost blond); and her sister Laetitia, (Teetie, destined to be a raven-haired beauty and I believe, a nun) and her sister Melanie (another blonde) ...

They constituted the distaff side of the progeny of Gerry Rhatigan and Helen Ryan (as they were always called by Mother's generation).

At an early count, there were also Eddie and Georgie (who had a way of aggravating my grandfather just by the way he called him 'Pawp').

With the exception of baseball, it was 'boys and girls together' for the variety of street games which occupied our time. The favorite was 'Babies', at which, when you think about it, girls would seem

119

natural. We usually played 'Babies' in the vacant lot next to our house. To get started, we all stood in a group and someone would be chosen to throw a rubber ball high against the side of the house. The rest could run off once the ball was thrown but then the thrower would yell someone's name and that person would have to come back, catch the ball, then shout, 'Stop!' and the rest of us would have to freeze in our tracks. The person would then try to hit someone with the ball -- if the throw was a success, the person hit would 'have a baby' and be out of the game. If the one throwing the ball missed, the baby would be his (or hers) and he'd be eliminated.

A variation was called '30 Seconds over Tokyo,' after the movie starring Spencer Tracy and Van Johnson. Talk about the war infiltrating our childish minds!

We also played stickball in the street which was fun but a bother because Van Woert was heavily trafficked.

Another 'boys only' game was 'baseball against the ledge.' The 'batter' would throw a rubber ball against the concrete steps leading up to the Rafferty house on the Dudley Park side of the street. If you hit the corner of the step just right, the ball would fly high across the street where the fielder would try to catch it for an out. If it hit the vacant house above him it was a home run; if it hit on one bounce, a triple; and so on.

A certain kind of pink rubber ball, available for 10 cents at Chet's on Swan Street on Arbor Hill, was particularly lively and perfect for ledge baseball. But tennis balls also fit the bill.

And horseshoes was popular. Not only were there were pits next to the Nehi factory, and horseshoes were very popular at the Dudley Park playground.

Hops and Pops

Big Tim Fitzgerald, was magical. He had 20-plus grandchildren and each sincerely believed he or she was his absolute favorite. It wasn't because he was a 'grampa' type. He wasn't. He was big, often gruff, and always busy. He was not only 'Pop' or 'Pops' within the family but also to half the kids on Van Woert Street. We all knew you could get his goat, for instance, by singing within his hearing range, "Pop, Pop, took a flop, In the garden, In a pot.'

He would fake -- I think -- a run at the culprit, feigning a kick, 'Damn it, if I catch you...'

But he never did. And he would respond the same if it were I or Georgie Rhatigan. These were the days before pooper scoopers and there lived a multitude of mutts in the neighborhood, so it was wise to develop a land-mine personality. Case in point: About half way up Swan Street hill, on the way to Arbor Hill, there was a shortcut leading off to the left, just before Goat Mountain, that led to Ten Broeck Street.

One day, Pop was taking the shortcut accompanied by brother Mike, perhaps 14 at the time.

'Darn it, Pop' Mike shouted, 'I just stepped in dog do!' He was standing there, one foot lifted.

'Don't worry about it, Michael.' Pop continued striding along. 'That's good luck.'

Mike took a couple of steps, stopped, considered, and went back to dip his other foot into the mess.

Among other things, Pop kept two or three gardens in the backyard. To the left was a garden plot, hedged by bridal wreath bushes on one side and backing up to the chicken coop, where he usually had six or seven hens and a rooster. There was a two- or three-foot path to walk past the flowers and on the other side was his vegetable garden -- by far the more important plot.

He grew corn, and tomatoes, and lettuce, and radishes, and carrots, and onions and beets. But never potatoes! Can anyone in class guess why?

And almost like his brood of offspring , the plants seemed blended into the hearty vibrations of the big Irishman, greening up tall and strong and hoping to gain his attention.

Pop's vegetable garden was always turned over, aerated, and well-watered. He knew about loam and humus and he had a couple of other secrets.

He worked for the City of Albany and had connections there. Every fall, a city dump truck would back into the lot next to our house and unload a huge pile of leaves which Pop would carefully spread and mix into the already rich soil..

That little bit of earth behind 98 Van Woert Street was also blessed by Pop's ingenuity.

In addition to the leaves, a city truck once a year would also dump off a load of hops which Pop would also use in the vegetable garden.

Talk about unaware! I always wondered from whither the hops. Pop would simply answer, 'The city.'

The leaves, yes, but hops?

So, there are those that would call it an epiphany when one day years after Pop's garden that it occurred to me.

Someone was telling a story about President Lyndon B. Johnson in the 1960s. He had just finished a presidential inspection at a naval base and a young officer was escorting him back to his conveyance. 'Sir,' he pointed 'that's your helicopter over there.'

'Son,' President Johnson said, 'they're all my helicopters.'

Bam, it came to me! You see, Uncle Dan O'Connell owned the City of Albany and that included the hometown Hedrick

Brewery. I'll bet you're getting it quicker than I did. Of course, why would O'Connell waste money buying trucks for Hedrick's when he had all he wanted lined up for him at the City garage?!

Son, he might say, they are all my trucks! And the hops, too.

Chapter 20
Sex Education

But about playing with the girls, you couldn't do that very long on warm Van Woert Street summer nights, without it becoming complicated. And so it was on one July evening in the early 40s that Elaine Rhatigan and I found ourselves alone in the Rogers backyard with a moon so bright you couldn't see the fireflies. At first we were a little nervous, then calmly with full complicity, and a degree of stomach flutters, at least on my part, we kissed.

And we did it again. I don't know how Elaine judged the occasion but for me at long last puberty had direction.

Elaine and I did quite a bit of that even after the Rhatigans, who had been living in the flat over the Milos family, moved to the former Dudley Observatory atop the hill which bordered Van Woert on the north side.

Mr. Rhatigan ' Gerry ' somehow landed a job as caretaker of the building, once an observatory. I think his wife, Helen Ryan, as everyone called her even after years of marriage and several children, had the connection with the O'Connell machine. Van Woert Street rules for young people frowned on bringing a person of the opposite sex into your house. Somehow, Daddy kind of became aware of Elaine. One night when we were in the kitchen, Daddy, under the mild influence of Stanton's half and half, said to me, 'You know you can't go wrong with an Irish girl ...' Turning to Mother, he added, 'Isn't that right, Nell"

'Oh, for God's sake!' Mother snapped. Although we did some petting, that was as far as most of us went. Guardian angels must have been busy because we knew precious little about sex, a subject never discussed in our homes, and that applied in all of the structures which wood-framed family existence on Van Woert Street.

A few years earlier when we were all about 9, June Allen from Second Street gave Bernard and me our first sex education class -- 'How a Woman Has a Baby 101.'

'They go into a hospital,' June had our

attention. 'There, they get on a cot and the doctor climbs on top and sticks his thing into her and the baby comes out of him and into her and then she has it.'

That left us blinking in disbelief. It was a rarity but Bernard and I agreed on something -- this couldn't be so.

Eventually Elaine Rhatigan started going with Jimmy Rafferty just out of the Army. A song popular summed it up for me, 'When I'm Not Near the Girl I Love, I Love the Girl I'm Near,' sung by David Wayne in 'Finian's Rainbow.' The girl I came to be near a lot was Betty Ballou, whose family moved into the house just across the street from ours. In it lived three sisters, Shirley, Betty, and Muriel (we called her Jean), all redheads of varying intensity. Shirley was tallish and thinnish with average red hair; Betty was more buxom and her hair lighter, and Jean's hair was auburn.

I had my first real date with Betty Ballou, whom to this day I remember as a wonderful, guileless human being.

I took a five-dollar bill from the jar where I kept my paper route savings. She got dressed up in a blue dress, splashed on

Lily of the Valley perfume and we headed off for downtown -- walking, of course. About a third of the way up Swan Street hill, we took 'the shortcut' which ran through some wilderness along a cliff over the brickyard on Van Woert on the left and beneath the backs of the houses on Colonie Street on the right. It led to Ten Broeck Street which in four or five blocks brought us to Clinton Avenue, just a block from the Palace and the Grand theaters downtown.

As I remember this particular date, we went to the Grand to see 'Golden Earrings' with Marlene Dietrich and Ray Milland ... Murvyn Vye (not the superstar La Dietrich) sang the title song, 'When your love wears golden earrings, she belongs to you.'

But before all that excitement, Betty and I stopped first at The Three Sisters ice cream parlor next to the Palace for Black and White Sundaes. This was a sundae served in a fancy 'silver' bowl which consisted of vanilla ice cream, covered in dark chocolate and whipped cream.

When we were not doing something as formal as going to the show, we would sit on the Ballous' front stoop and neck. Even that had to be done in the context of a game. If a car came up or down the street with only one light, you would shout 'Fididdle.' If the girl said it first, she got to whack you one in the face; if the boy was first, he would get a kiss. Occupying the stoop normally would be Betty and I and Puggy and Jean.

A Fitzgerald by Any Name

My Aunt Mary, her husband Joker Waters, and my cousins Jack and Joan lived next door to us at 94 Van Woert. Almost everyone had seen 'Going My Way,' the Leo McCary movie which proved that Bing Crosby could act as well as sing. And we all were crazy about impish Barry Fitzgerald. Then one night at the Waterses, cousin Joan, Elaine Rhatigan and I sat stunned into silence, when somebody on the radio mentioned that Barry wasn't Catholic. Damn! And I had hoped we were relatives. But he wasn't even a Fitzgerald -- he and Arthur Shields were real-life brothers.

The movie featured a subplot involving

the Metropolitan Opera and it was then
that many of us fell in love with 'Carmen' -
- or was it Rise Stevens?

Chapter 21
The Names Game

When I was young, everyone in the family called me 'Junior,' and I was deathly afraid that nickname might reach the street. I finally brought up the subject with Daddy. 'I can understand,' he rasped. 'But what should we call you -- there can't be two Carmens.'

I never thought to interject that there wouldn't be two Carmens, he was either Jinx or Daddy ... only strangers and Italians called him Carmen.

'Well, maybe some other nickname,' I said. He sat at the kitchen table, his fingertips twisting in the hair at the side of his head. 'I got it,' he said, 'how about Studs?' James Farrell's fictional hero 'Studs Lonigan' was popular at the time. I looked at him oddly. 'It's from a book,' he said, 'haven't you ever heard of 'Studs Lonigan?' asked the native of Bellona, Italy.

At least he didn't propose Horatio Alger,

another of his literary favorites.

We eventually agreed on 'Butch.' With my stubborn refusal to answer to 'Junior,' that name soon vanished and was replaced by Butch -- but only in the family. On the streets, I maintained Carmen status.

The subject arose again in a couple of years when I was confirmed. Daddy assumed I would pick his middle name, Anthony. And he was hurt when I told him I had decided on John.

'But then you won't be junior any more,' he said. My look told him that's what I intended. His look told me I had wounded him.

Brother Mike stood up for me at Confirmation, and gave me a pocket Mickey Mouse watch (I wondered if he thought that character summed up the significance of the sacrament) And I was Carmen J. Viglucci, period. Well, Butch, too.

Chapter 22
The Cousins
Fitzgerald and Viglucci

The children and grandchildren of Timothy (Pop) Fitzgerald and Delia (Ma) Gilligan born one or two years apart beginning in 1898.

Mary Fitzgerald Waters, born 1898, wed to John (Joker) Waters;
Children: John (Jackie), Joan.

John Fitzgerald, born 1899, killed in France, Sept. 28, 1918.

James Fitzgerald, born 1901, wed to Mary Smith; Children Mary, Patricia

Margaret, born 1903 (twin was stillborn), wed to Michael (Mickey) Regan;
Children: Helen, John (Jackie), Michael (Mickey)
Helen Fitzgerald, born 1905, wed to Carmen (Jinx) Viglucci
Children: Michael, Andrew, Carmen, Helen

(Honey);

Timothy Fitzgerald wed to Margaret Lacey;
Children: Timothy, James, John, Edward (or as we referred to them: Timmy-Jimmy-Johnny-and-Ed

Nancy Fitzgerald wed to Stephen Fiato;
Children: Joseph (Joey), Marilyn, Stephen, Timothy (Timmie)

Elizabeth Fitzgerald (Bessie) wed to Charles (Charlie) Young;
Children: Shirley, Elizabeth (Betty), Audrey

Dennis Fitzgerald (Dinny), born 1912, wed to Mildred Donahue;
Children: Dennis (Denny), Matthew (Matt)
Catherine Fitzgerald (Kate) wed to Frank Cardamone;
Children: Frances, Thomas (Tommy)

The children and grandchildren of Michele Vigliucci and Carmela (Aurelio) Vigliucci :

Carmen A. Viglucci wed to Helen Viglucci.
Their children: Mike, Andrew, Carmen,
Helen (Honey).
Josephine wed to Frank Martello;
(Josephine later remarried.) Their
children: Augie and Frances.
  Genevieve wed to Sam LoGiudice. Their
children: Connie, Joe, Mela, Sam, Mary
Ann.

Chapter 23

Mystery of Lumbago

The oldest of the 25 'Fitzgerald' cousins was John L. (Jack) Waters, widely and respectably known as 'The Jeep.' I'm not sure where he got the nickname nor do I know if he was named for his mother Mary's brother killed in World War I or for his father, also John, but mainly called Joker.

For a long time the Waterses lived in the next house toward the Hudson from us, No. 94, though we were separated by a vacant lot mostly used by Tom Lacey for his wood business.

'Pop is okay,' the older and wiser Jeep chuckled one day, 'though a bit on the excitable side.'

The two had a strange rapport. Case in point: One day when Jeep was probably about 15, he was sawing a board in our backyard, his sandy-colored, straight hair flopping in his eyes in rhythm with his motion, when he suddenly caused a terrible screech.

'Goddamn it, Waters,' our grandfather

yelled out the back window. 'You're sawing through a nail!'

'It's okay, Pop,' Jeep said soothingly, 'I'm almost through it now.'

Jeep had an entirely different viewpoint on Jinx. 'The man's got eyes in the back of his head,' he cautioned me one day. 'If you're trying to pull something, be careful around Uncle Jinx.'

This was true. But sometimes Daddy could be had. Once, we dug a hole in the far reaches of the backyard near the clubhouse.

This was no mere dent in the ground; it was fully six feet deep and two, maybe three, of us could stand in at once and with a rock underfoot stare out undetected over the environs from the back of the houses on Van Woert, up to the Colonie Street dumps on the other side. We named the hole Lumbago; Jackie Regan more than likely providing the creativity as he had a way with names. Shortly after the hole was finished, Daddy in his uncanny way, came home using the shortcut from Swan Street to our backyard. This was unusual for a number of reasons -- first, Daddy seldom arrived home on foot (Mother would say Daddy seldom arrived home period); if he had to walk he never took a shortcut through weeds; and he was hardly ever in the far reaches of the backyard.

Yet, one day while Lumbago was still a freshly dug hole, along came Daddy; he noticed the pile of dirt; he spotted the hole; and he ordered us to fill it up.

A 'revoltin' development,' as Jimmy Durante would say. So we sawed some boards, wedged them in about a foot beneath the surface and covered them with dirt; carted away the excess dirt to the stretch of weed-covered lots Bernard and I called Hispaniola. Then we waited. Never volunteer information in this kind of situation; it's a giveaway.

Finally, one day Daddy asked me if we filled in the hole. 'Yes.' I wasn't lying, it was only a mental reservation (to understand this term, look up Sisters of Charity). He didn't question further and I don't think he ever double-checked.

Almost Paradise

'Don't ever hate anyone because of his nationality or race,' Daddy said. 'You'll hear some people, maybe in your own family, say bigoted things about the Jews, or colored people or others. They're all wrong, understand?Everybody's the same.'
'Okay,' I said.
There was a pause then daddy continued, 'Except the French.'

Harry Warren
Who's the Bigot!

In the late Thirties, there was a ditty which I thought for years was poking mean fun at Italian immigrants. It was called 'Where Do You Worka, John?' and to this day I can remember a guy singing in 'pidgin' English, *Where do you worka, John? The Delaware Lackawann; And waddya doa, John? I poosh, I poosh, I poosh, And where do you poosha, John? On the Delaware Lackawann, awan, awan, awan the Delaware Lackawann.*

The next stanza begins with a soprano's voice, *'Where do you worka, Marie? The telephone company ; And waddya doa, Marie? I poosh, I poosh, I poosh. And where do you poosha, Marie?At the telephone company, any, any, any, the telephone company.'*

In my juvenile mind's eye, I could picture some white Anglo-Saxon Protestant bigot, the kind that convicted Sacco and Vanzetti, sitting back and mocking the dumb dagoes and making money at the same time.

What a surprise it was for me to learn many years later that the song was written by famous Hollywood and Broadway composer Harry Warren. Finding out that a legitimate musical talent wrote 'Where Do You Worka, John?' was unexpected, so it was a 'catastastroke' in Durante English to learn that Harry Warren was only a stage name. The composer's real name was Salvatore Anthony Guaragna!

These twists can only happen to the kind of person who sees a bigot behind every tree -- would that be a bigo-tree? And just who was the bigot in this scenario?!

Not only did Warren write the Italian ditty; but from 1932 to 1957, he composed more songs than anyone who made the top ten of radio's most famous musical show, 'The Hit Parade.' In those 15 years, 42 Warren songs were among the top ten and 21 of them were No. 1. Guess what composer finished second to Warren? Irving Berlin, that's who! Warren was nominated 11 times in the Academy Award's Best Song category, winning the Oscar three times ' for the swinging 'Lullaby of Broadway,' from 'Gold Diggers of 1935,' in 1935; the misty 'You'll Never Know,' perhaps the most sentimental love ballad of World War II; done by the legendary Alice Faye in 'Hello, Frisco, Hello' in 1943, and 'On the Atchison, Topeka and the Santa Fe,' sung by none other than Judy Garland in 'The Harvey Girls' in 1946.

Mr. Warren, uh, make that Signore Guaragna, also wrote the first song ever to win a Gold Record 'Chattanooga Choo Choo,' recorded by America's top big band, the Glen Miller Orchestra.

And Warren fought the Great Depression in his way. His song, 'We're in the Money,' was a major morale-builder in the mid 30s.

It is to be noted, that Warren seldom did lyrics but he wrote the music to all these songs.

Another interesting note about Warren and his long career. 'That's Amore,' a song he wrote for Dean Martin in his 1953 movie with Jerry Lewis, 'The Caddy,' re-surfaced in 1987's 'Moonstruck', again sung by Dino and for which Cher and Olympia Dukakis won Academy Awards. That, dear friends, is a gap of 34 years. Talk about staying power!

I particularly honor the monumental work of this great American composer because two of his songs bring memories of two of the dearest ladies in my life, my mother and my forever young aunt Catherine. More than one morning while rubbing sleep out of my eyes coming down the stairs I could hear Mother whistling over her ironing, and often it was one of her favorite songs, 'I'll Get By,' another Warren masterpiece. I don't know if Mother tied in the lyrics with her life with Jinx (one line states 'poverty may come my way, it's true') but I sense that ' I Had the Craziest Dream' (yes, another Warren song) definitely reminded Kate of her 'Full Blooded Italian' husband Frank Cardamone.

Here are some other Salvatore Anthony Guaragna songs, Which are your favorites?

About a Quarter to Nine
An Affair to Remember (the Cary Grant-Deborah Kerr gem)
At Last
Boulevard of Broken Dreams (with the oh-so melancholy line 'We laugh tonight and cry tomorrow')
Forty-Second Street
Friendly Star
Million Dollar Baby in a Five and Ten Cent Store
I Love My Baby, My Baby Loves Me
Yi, Yi, Yi Yi, I Love You Very Much (for the South American bombshell Carmen Miranda)
I'll String along with you
I'm a Lone Cowhand from the Rio Grand
It's a Big, Wide Wonderful World
Jeepers Creepers
Love Is Where You Find It
Lulu's Back in town

Marty
The More I See You
My Dream Is Yours
No Love, No Nothing' ('until my baby comes home')
She's a Latin from Manhattan
This Heart of Mine
You Must Have Been a Beautiful Baby
You Wonderful You
You're My Everything

Chapter 24
Verboten!

I wasn't always so fortunate in dealing with Daddy as I was concerning Lumbago. Two things he hated more than the French -- guns and bicycles. One night in a crap game, I won a single-shot 22 rifle from Puggy La Mountain.

At home, we had a floor-to-ceiling, two-door cupboard in the kitchen. In the back, far to the right, I kept the jar with my paper route money behind a broken and loose board -- either gnawing rats caused it or Pop made it in an ingenious effort to keep them out. With a couple of tugs I managed to make it a wider slot and slid my .22 in there.

On special occasions, such as going shooting down near Normans Kill Creek with my school buddy Fred Weber, I could easily remove it.

Things went swimmingly for quite some time until one day I came crashing through the kitchen door and what I saw brought me to a skidding halt.

There was Daddy, sitting at the kitchen table, playing his role -- arms crossed over suspender-covered undershirt. On the table was my single-shot .22.

'What'd you do, buy a gun?' was the best I could do on such short notice.

'Nooo,' he drew the word out.

'Where'd you get it?' I asked wide-eyed.

'Guess,' he said.

I had to confess and promise to get rid of it. Did I? What do you think?

Even more anathema than guns were bicycles. Through his experiences as a cab driver, Daddy was convinced bicyclists had no place in our streets. So I never had a bike until the day Billy Villeneuve was selling his. We made a deal, I'd pay him five dollars, the bike would be mine, but he'd keep it at his house and swear it was his if you-know-who ever investigated.

I have to preface this upcoming pedaling experience with mention that one dull Sunday afternoon, Billy Rafferty, Richie Cox, and I decided to take a walk to kill time and ended up nine miles away at the airport. That's a story in itself but here it serves to note that we had learned the way to the airport -- and one day it seemed like a good idea to bike there. Somewhere out on West Sand Lake Road, three of us were pedaling along in single-file fashion, safely to the side of the road, when some idiot driver started honking his horn. I waved him by but the car stayed right there, positioned at 7 o'clock. The horn blew again. I waved exasperatedly. When the horn blew again, I turned to cast an epithet and there crouched for better vision of his prey was Daddy in the cockpit of his Albany Quarter Cab. He sped by, shouting out the window, 'I'll see you home.' Talk about ruining your day!

My defense, 'I know you said I couldn't own a bike, but I didn't know you meant I couldn't ride one' -- worked somewhat. But considering Daddy's profession at the time, I didn't get to use the bike very often.

Sevens Up

The seven deadly sins are Envy, Greed, Sloth, Gluttony, Lust, Anger and Hate... The seven dwarfs are Grumpy, Happy,

Doc, Bashful, Sneezy, Sleepy and Dopey...
The Fordham seven blocks of granite are
Vince Lombardi, Al Bart, John Druze,
Harry Jacunski, Leo Paquin, Nat Pierce,
Alex Wojciechowicz, Ed Franco.
The seven little Foys are Bryan W.,
Charley, Dick, Eddie Jr., Irving, Madeline,
and Mary.
The Seven Sacraments of the Roman
Catholic Church are (or were) Baptism,
Confirmation, Holy Eucharist, Penance,
Extreme Unction, Holy Orders, and
Matrimony.
And my seven teachers at St. Joseph, in
order of ascendancy, Grades 1-7, were
Sister Winifred, Sister Josepha, Sister
Mary Magdalen, Sister Claire, Sister
Domenica, Sister Alice, and Miss Carey.

Chapter 25
Regiment of Nuns

St. Joseph's Academy stood at the corner of Second and Swan streets, crowning Arbor Hill. The building still stands even though it already was old in 1938. At one time, Pop said, it was the Christian Brothers school which he attended ('Now the Brothers knew how to handle tough guys.') Later it was to become the parochial school.

The principal was Sister Mary, kind of the Wicked Witch of the top floor.

One seldom saw Sister Mary and one certainly was happy of that. There was little reason for a sister to send anyone to her office; each was quite capable of administering her own, shall we say, justice.

Years later when I entered the Army of the United States, the transition from civilian life was easier for me than most. After the regimentation of the good Sisters of Charity, the Army, Korean War thrown in, was a walk in the park. The Army liked us not to think, just react as extensive, repetitive training had taught us. It's quite possible, I'm sure, the Army adapted these tactics from St. Joseph's.

The sisters of Charity were distinctive in other ways. Their headdresses called cornets or cornettes seemed liked ship's sails. (Think of the Flying Nun.)The large white winged head covering, worn back in the Forties, was not only unique but capable of instilling respect upon sight— and maybe a little trepidation, although not fear.

You might be interested to know that the cornette was a piece of female headwear that was especially popular in Europe in the 15th to 17th century. It consisted of a large starched piece of white cloth folded upwards in such a way as to create the resemblance of horns on the wearer's head. St. Vincent de Paul who founded the order wanted the sisters to resemble ordinary middle-class women as much as possible in their clothing. The sisters abandoned the cornette in 1964.

Lunch was not served at school; thus we all walked the distance there in the morning, back home at noon, and back to school in the afternoon.

If we were to take part in a program at the church, down Second Street to Ten Broeck, we marched in class groups. We followed this procedure any time we were out in the field, whether to the Pruyn Library at Clinton and Pearl or to a wake. At kindergarten at School 8 back on Madison Avenue in the South End, education went swimmingly. Miss Dooley read to us, we got to hold little girls' hands doing 'Ring around the Rosey,' played with blocks and when nature called, we merely raised pudgy little hands and went off. School was just peachy.

Things were to change dramatically. In the summer of 1938 we moved to Van Woert from Grand Street and Mother enrolled me in St. Joseph's Academy.

My first nun was Sister Winifred, tall and stern, her cornet high on her head, our first grade teacher. House rules: We all went to urinate at 10:30 a.m. and again at 2:30 p.m. -- whether we had to or not. And we could not go at any other time.

The boys room was in the basement and mainly consisted of a long trough against the wall, where we all stood elbow to elbow and peed in unison. We behaved because in the doorway was Sister Winifred, discreetly, we hoped, overseeing all activity.

No. 1: This didn't work for me. One day, unable to contain myself until 10:30 and after being rebuked by Sister Winifred for seeking relief, I went right there, sitting at my desk. The sister was coldly angry. With great disdain, she pointed out my personal puddle to the whole class. Sympathy? I can still see all my peers, clucking their tongues and slowly shaking their heads in synch with their holy leader.

No. 2: This was another story. I would try my best to be a man; saying the recess prayer with the class, slowly marching in line through the hall, down the stairs, out onto Swan Street and then taking off like a cramped lemming across Arbor Hill, Second Street, Third Street, Livingston Avenue, Colonie Street -- three times I didn't make it. But eventually I adjusted to the Sisters' schedule.

On the bright side of the first grade, were Jane Farley (freckle face), Patricia Kelly (long blonde tubes done with a curling

iron) and dark-haired Rosemary Krusik --
six-year-olds do notice.

Second grade, Sister Josepha. Respite. A
very pleasant, gentle old lady. Mother also
had her in the second grade.

In the third grade, Sister Mary Magdalen,
one of the younger and maybe even
pretty, sisters, taught us, besides Religion,
some excruciating methods of torture.
Once, she heard one of the boys swear
when we went to the bathroom. She
accused me. I didn't do it but, as I was to
learn, denial amounted to conviction with
the Sisters of Charity.

First, she squeezed the back of my neck
with her surprisingly strong fingers:
'That's for swearing,' she said.

'Now for lying, stand on top of your desk,'
she ordered. I did so, shaking. 'Raise your
hands above your head -- higher!'

She left me like that as the class
continued. Try it, it hurts. And cursing and
lying weren't even among the seven
deadly sins.

It's a matter of conjecture but it's possible
Sister Mary Magdalen would endorse
waterboarding, if squeezing the neck
didn't always work.

Later in the year 1942, Jane Farley and her auburn hair and freckles all died. They said that the doctors misdiagnosed a bursting appendix for what we called 'the grippe.' One afternoon, Sister Mary Magdalen marched the class over to(I'm almost certain) First Street, for Jane's wake. There she was, laid out in a frilly, long peach-colored dress, dead at 8. Later in the day, Sister gave us an assignment: write a brief piece on how we would remember Jane Farley.

'Smiling,' I wrote, short and to the point. When the Sister later approached me with my paper in her hand, I felt the back of my neck start to tighten up.

'Very good job,' she said, handing it back. I couldn't get over it. I looked at it again, turned it sideways, upside down. 'Very good job,' I repeated to myself. 'Maybe someday I'll be a writer.'

Jane Farley was my second corpse. Ma, my Strand Theater grandmother, had died on Dec. 8, 1940.

Her wake naturally was at 98 Van Woert, the same house, the same room, where her son Jack Fitzgerald was shipped home in a box from France in 1919.

Despite a cold, blizzardy night, with all the relatives and Van Woert Streeters the house was full during Ma's calling hours. Was I surprised when Sister Mary Magdalen showed up, accompanied, of course, as nuns always were in those days, by another Sister. We were very impressed to think that a Sister would go to this trouble. I was wondering if she knew Ma was my grandmother but after the two sisters knelt side by side at the casket to pray, she asked someone, 'Is Carmen here?'

I was pointed out and she looked at me. Her face held a kind expression which I had not seen before. She then gathered her shawls and cloaks and skirts and other things together and left.

My curiosity went into overgear -- was it just a tradition for Sisters to visit a dead person? Did they take the load off the priests, who probably only went to wakes of better-off folks? I want to quickly absolve our pastor, Father Michael Looney, from that slight. He was really too old and tottering to perform such duties. In fact, this would be the place to mention that I recall about a year later going with

Mother to visit Father Looney at his rectory on St. Joseph's Terrace, at the corner of Second Street. I believe it must have been to arrange a first anniversary Mass for Ma. We sat in a dark, musty office. Father Looney was tall, stoop-shouldered, with pale, almost translucent blue eyes which seemed to have trouble focusing.

'It boggles my mind,' he muttered so low we had to strain to hear him. 'For some reason, God always takes folks so young' (that's what he said, although Ma was 66, considered old in those days). 'And here I am. Every night before I nod off I pray that He take me. Yet every morning I wake up again.'

More than once, he collapsed on the altar during Mass at St. Joseph's Church. Finally, one time, he didn't get up. God had granted his wish.

Attending Ma's wake was not the only unforgettable thing about Mary Magdalen. On another day, she took the class on a walk, almost as significant as the visit to Jane Farley. Down Second Street, over Ten Broeck, left on Clinton, past the Palace which regularly played MGM movies. She took us to the John V. L. Pruyn Library. We didn't have a library at SJA, so this was extremely important. For most of the kids, it was our first visit to a library. We were thrilled and when we all got borrowing cards, it was a highlight of our lives.

The first book I withdrew was 'He Went with Vasco Da Gama,' by Louise A. Kent. Next time, it was her "He went with Marco Polo." (More on Marco later.) Obviously they made an impression—so much so that a couple of years ago I went hunting on the internet for used copies and now have them on my bookshelves.

I have to admit that despite her sadistic tendencies, Sister Mary Magdalen still holds a special place in my heart. Not only because she visited Ma, but because much as with Jane Farley, I remember her smiling, too.

Amedeo Obici
More Than Peanuts

Back in the Preface of this kaleidoscopic message, I mentioned something about Mr. Peanut being the most important person who ever visited our neighborhood school, St. Joseph's Academy, at Second and Swan streets in Albany. N.Y.

In case you didn't know it, I was setting you up for this chapter. So if you didn't read it before, you better skedaddle back to it now. There is a lot more to Mr. Peanut than you may know or not.

He is a figurative ancestor for many Italian-Americans. Let's start at the beginning.

Amedeo Obici was born in 1876 in a small town in Italy, way up in the northeast near Venice. He came over to this land of milk, honey and Budweiser at the age of 11. He knew no English and became a fruit-stand vendor in the dusty coal-mining city of Scranton, Pa. Then he moved to neighboring Wilkes-Barre (Albany Senators fans, does this remind you of the 1940s Eastern League, including those two teams, the Miners and the Barons?) In Wilkes-Barre, Obici got himself a horse and wagon, dubbed himself the Peanut Specialist, and rode around town making a living.

A comic character? Not worthy of elaboration? Don't kid yourself.

Soon he developed his own method of blanching whole roasted peanuts and had six employees and some crude machinery. In 1906, he went into partnership with Mario Peruzzi, and you probably figured out by now, he was on his way to establishing Planter's Peanuts. Obici had an idea to begin selling his peanuts in a small cellophane bag across the nation. A doubter told him, 'Du zay pazz?' (you're crazy!) You gonna sell peanuts in a little bag for five cents? How many bags you gotta sell to make any money?

Probably only Obici knew the answer. But however many bags it took, he sold them. But there's more.

Not only did Obici create the mechanics of his business, he also masterminded the marketing. If you happened to go to St. Joseph's Academy, you know about Mr. Peanut. In 1916, Obici introduced this promotional character, based on the original drawing of a 14-year-old boy. Gradually, Mr. Peanut added a top hat, white spats, ebony cane, and a monocle to his unique ensemble. It was to become one of America's most successful advertising ploys. Ask the kids at S.J.A. When he visited, he would pass out rectangular black and white drawings of himself. You stared real hard at the picture for some seconds, then stare at the blackboard where he would be reproduced from our retinas 'and our memories' forever!

Anyway, Mr. Peanut was an annual tradition at St. Joseph's. Another was 'the Filipino,' who would bring his bag of yoyo tricks and set up shop on Swan Street to catch us kids coming to and fro school. Then there was the photographer who showed up with a black and white pony and took photos of kids on horseback, the proofs showing up at our houses. Depression and all, they were difficult to ignore by parents. Mine ended up in the dining room closet.

Ah, yes, The Filipino; Mr. Peanut; the Pony. Whatever happened to Santa?

Chapter 26
Queen of the May

St. Joseph's was coed, but the boys and girls sat apart -- or at least as separate as the Sisters could get us. Usually, the girls sat in the first three rows; the boys in the next three. The boys had no dress code but the girls wore uniforms. Plaid skirts, dark sweaters and starched, removable white collars.

Most grades had two classes -- the A group and the B group -- knowing the sisters' penchant for embarrassment as an educational tool, it's easy to figure who was who. To carry this tactic further, the kids with the better grades would sit toward the front of the class; the lesser the marks the farther back you sat.

Each day, class, morning and afternoon, started and ended with prayers. Usually they were just routine. But once in a while, they were pointed.

In our class were two 'colored' sisters (siblings, not nuns, that is). When 'black is beautiful' gained ascendancy, it became unacceptable to call people 'colored' but back at that time it was considered respectable. It certainly was preferable to some of the other choices.

Although not Catholic the parents of the two black girls felt the discipline of St. Joseph's would be good for them. Talk about a bad move!

One day, one of the sisters decided to send our prayers into more direct action.

'Today, children, we are going to pray for the Johnson girls' (author's note: not their real name). 'We know that because they are Protestant they may not be going to heaven. Please, girls, stand up.'

This is not an exact quote, but the gist of her comment. She didn't realize her prejudice.

The pair stood there fumbling with their hands as we then said a couple of Hail Marys for them. The Sister added: 'Let's pray that the Lord takes them under His wing.'

She didn't mean that He might take them into heaven, she meant that He might make them become Catholics. Now, Sister may have been somewhat obnoxious in her delivery but by no means was she alone in that belief; many of our teachers and priests were equally ignorant.

In fact, in the 40s, an American Jesuit, Father Leonard Feeney, proclaimed that no non-Catholic could be saved. Even though he was chastised by the Church and eventually excommunicated during the papacy of Pius XII in 1953, Feeney's followers persisted in championing his claim.

To quote from the Baltimore Catechism from the sixties with the Imprimatur of Francis Cardinal Spellman: 'When we say 'outside the Church there is no salvation,' we mean that those who through their own grave fault do not know that the Catholic Church is the true Church, or who, knowing it, refuse to join it, cannot be saved.'

Years later, Bishop Sheen would remember such puffery: 'A man died and went to Heaven,' Sheen said on television. 'St. Peter showed him about. When they came to the first section, Peter said, 'Here is where all the Protestants live.' A short time later, he pointed out another section, 'And here is where all the Jews are.' At the third section, he said, 'And here is where all the Catholics are ... shhh, they think they're the only ones here.'

Bishop Sheen, where were you when we needed you?

One of the big events of the year at St. Joseph's was May Day. A giant production featured the crowning of Mary Queen of the May. Everybody in school took part, including a procession down Second Street from the school to the church. The girls wore bridal attendants' gowns except for one who would play Mary -- obviously the star of the play. Everyone would march, even the parish priests, at the head of the parade obviously. We weren't too versed in the Bible maybe our parish leaders had never heard of 'the last shall be first.'

We would practice weeks for the May Day parade which ended up with an elaborate ceremony inside the packed church.

One year I was a page boy -- had to wear a blue silk outfit, with white silk stockings and carry a sword, which was really a piece of wood, coated with glue and covered with silver sprinkles. The page boys' main chore came on the altar when 'Mary' would walk between raised swords to the hymn, 'O, Mary, we crown thee with blossoms today, queen of the angels, queen of the May!'

Every year we were asked to give money for the missions. As always, the Sisters made a contest of it. They would make a big graph, set it up in the front of the room. Each row would have its own bar in a different color and every Friday our contributions would be added and the row extended toward a prescribed goal. I noticed that the kids who brought in the most dough also did fairly well on their tests. Do you think? Nah!

St. Joseph's Church

The Gothic Revival structure   on Ten Broeck Street was built for the growing Irish immigrant population in the northern neighborhoods of Albany. It was finished in 1860 and has served as the district's focal point ever since.

The Catholic diocese of Albany stopped using St. Joseph's Church in 1994; since then there have been various efforts to restore it. But in my mind it remains a landmark of school day memories. Our school, St. Joseph's Academy, was two blocks away.

We sometimes were marched from school to St. Joseph's church for special occasions-- for example, Lenten services. The kneelers gave the Sisters a perfect mechanism for punishment. Do something wrong, speak out of turn, speak in turn, and soon you would be kneeling for an open-ended period as penalty.

To get even, when so chastised some of us would kneel on one knee 'to show her.' To this day, I still do this during Mass.

Sister Domenica, fifth grade, was another easy-going teacher. She must have liked me because she designated me an eraser clapper. The fifth grade windowed onto a roof of a lower level of the school, toward the First Street end. So we would climb out the window onto the roof, bang the erasers together, let the chalk dust fly and with it the school hours.

Chapter 27
Sister on Attack!

One Sister brought a Scottish burr with her to the sixth grade and was the first sister whose reputation had preceded her. How bad could she be, we wondered' And we found out.

One day, we were all reading aloud together about Marco Polo when Sister Alice interrupted and asked: 'Now where did Marco Polo go?'

I knew the answer because by this time I had read 'He Went with Marco Polo,' another in author Kent's series. Besides the answer was common knowledge, so I answered sarcastically, 'Sing Sing?'

For this, I was summarily expelled from school by Sister Alice, sent home with a note which said that I could not return unless accompanied by a parent.

I sat on the hill behind our house and waited until I saw Mother leave for work at the Federal Bakery downstreet. When she left, about 11:30, I went home. Imagine my surprise upon rushing in the back door and finding Daddy there. I don't know why he wasn't at work, but there he was.

'What are you doing here?' I asked.

'I could ask you the same thing,' he rasped. There was no use sparring around; I simply told him what had happened.

'You going back with me?' I asked, dreading the idea.

'No,' Daddy said. 'I'm going to send a note back with you instead.' He wrote on the other side of her message: 'Dear Sister, develop a sense of humor.'

I knew this might be war but I was trapped. And I was happy that Daddy wasn't returning with me. I went back, and handed it to her. She read it straight-faced, crumpled it in a ball and threw it in the waste basket, never to refer to it again. I was back but by no means was I off the hook. From then on, whenever I did something of which she disapproved, she would exile me to the cloakroom or worse make me sit in the kneehole of her desk. There I'd be, all cramped up looking at Sister's dark skirts and ducking as she swung her ankle-high black boots around beneath the desk.

Though we were 6-A, for some reason,

some of the real non-academic kids were in our room, just waiting to be 16 so they could get out. Maybe, the Sister had particular success with the older children. One such was a Polish boy, first name Ziggy, who was extremely shy which seemed to be most of his problem. He had a multisyllabic last name, one with piles of consonants, mostly Zs, which was hard to spell.

When things would get dull for Sister, she liked to turn on Ziggy. 'Stand on your feet,' she would begin and we would all cringe. 'Spell your last name,' she would say. Ziggy, who had curly blond hair, clear blue eyes and a great complexion, would begin to shuffle, his face turning purple. He would try, and fail. She would order him to try again. Kids can be cruel but this was too much for even us. When his face would show signs of crumbling into tears, she would say something like, 'Sit down ... why do I even try?'

Sister also was prone to hit -- with her hand, her fist, a ruler, a pointer -- anything available. Other nuns also used to crack our knuckles with a ruler, but Sister would turn it sideways so the sharp edge could cut. She also liked to bash heads against the blackboard.

 Zack was the only kid in the sixth grade with five o'clock shadow. While we might get in trouble for chewing gum, Zack would be disciplined for wearing a cigarette behind his ear.

One day Sister was trying to humiliate Zack who didn't humiliate. She got so frustrated she smacked him in the face. In a flash reflex, he responded in kind, hitting her face lightly.

We sat stunned. Every mouth must have gaped the same measured opening in Catholic school cadence. Complete silence as Sister stared at Zack.

Then someone in the back started it -- a gentle, lone clapping. Soon came a smattering of applause. Zack left, never to return, to my knowledge.

My sister Honey also started at St. Joseph's. I remember taking her collars to Soon Lee, the Chinese launderer in the basement at First and Swan, just next to the school.

She had a similar problem to mine in the first grade. But she had a medical reason -- some kind of bladder infection was forcing her to go to the bathroom often and Sister wouldn't allow it.

Mother sent a note with Honey asking a dispensation. Sister Winifred said that she didn't have the authority to bend the rules; that Mother would have to take it up with Sister Mary. That was usually enough to end such matters, but the Sisters of Charity did not know Helen Frances (Nell)Fitzgerald who quickly made an appointment with Sister Mary. Nearby St. Joseph's on Third Street was School 6. Arbor Hill was mostly black and the kids almost all went to '6.' When the sisters wanted to scare you they would threaten you with expulsion, adding, 'And you'll end up at School 6.' To them it must have seemed a fate worse than hell full of all those Protestants, mostly black ones at that.

When Mother sat down with Honey at her side, Sister Mary was cold and precise.

'We just don't break rules for one child.'

Mother was stubborn, too.

'Then she won't come to school any more.'

'Fine,' Sister Mary smiled triumphantly, 'I can sign transfer papers for her to School 6.'

'Go ahead,' my mother said, to her everlasting glory.

'What?' Sister Mary was stunned.

'Sign the papers,' Mother said, fluttering her hand at the principal. 'Now! I don't want my daughter associating with the likes of you.'

So Honey started at School 6 and her problem soon disappeared. I never knew how. Perhaps there was an emotional component to her urgent bathroom visits. Whatever, the reason, Mother deserved the credit.

The seventh grade we had a lay teacher. Miss Carey was considered a fuss budget, but she was a kind lady. Unfortunately, she dyed her hair which gave rise to the song (tune of 'After the Ball'):

'After the class was over,
Miss Carey took off her glass eye,
Put her pegleg in the corner,
Hung her hair up to dry.'

Deflation!

On the last day of school after finishing sixth grade, Bernard and I decided to celebrate by going downstreet to the

Strand to see 'Crash Dive,' a submarine movie starring Tyrone Power and Dana Andrews. We were carrying our report cards in brown manila envelopes.

At Ten Broeck and Clinton Avenue, a gray-haired woman stopped us and asked about the envelopes. When we showed her our report cards, she dipped into a little change purse, saying, 'You both deserve dimes' and she handed us coins. At the candy stand inside the show, my 'dime' turned out to be a 'silver' penny -- damn the war! But Bernard indeed had a dime. He shared his Milk Duds -- after all, what are friends for?

Chapter 28
Fire Strikes School!

As if marching to and fro all over the old building and Arbor Hill wasn't enough, we regularly had fire drills. On Monday, Jan. 15, 1945, the fire bell rang. Seven A was on an upper floor, probably the third. Like the good little soldiers we were, we got up, fell in, and marched as the old bell gonged away.

'Why do they always have drills on cold days?' someone asked just as someone else said, 'Is that smoke?'

By the time we reached the stairwells, the smoke was all around us. No one panicked (thank you, Sisters), and though two firemen were hurt, not one child was injured as we made our way out of the fire that was to gut St. Joseph's and put it out of commission for years.

'Two Overcome Battling Flames; Chief Made Ill' ran the Page 1 headline in the Knick News. A page 1 photo showed some of the Sisters of Charity in their white-winged cornets and some pupils watching the blaze. The cutline described the 'spectacular fire that forced 700 pupils to the street.'

Victor Rolando was in the seventh grade; his father was Renato Rolando, the parish organist, and lived on Ten Broeck Place, only two or three football fields from the school. Victor ran home to tell his father who at first didn't believe him and began to take him back to school until they saw the smoke and the fire trucks...

We stood in the cold and watched the firemen fight the blaze.

'Oh, my God,' I think it was Richie Cox exclaiming, 'Meathead skipped today.' Trouble. 'Meathead' was a nickname Bernard Milos couldn't escape because of his ferocious acne.

We knew he wouldn't be at Hayes soda fountain, or Chet's, or Johnny McAleer's -- all were too close to the school.

'He must have gone downstreet, maybe a show,' someone said. We had left our coats in the fire and it was a frigid day so we couldn't search too far.

On the way home, we checked the stores -- Joel Levine's, Sadie's, and Mr. Campbell's. No Bernard. We stayed out as best we could, hoping to catch him before he got home.

'He'll be all right,' Eddie Rhatigan said, 'he'll hear about it.'

But he didn't, not in time, that is. He had gone to the show and arranged to get home at around 4. His fatal mistake: He took a shortcut near the dumps instead of coming up the street where we were waiting.

Big Bertha, as we called Mrs. Milos behind her back and when Bernard wasn't around, flashed an unusually bright smile at her son as he came in the house.

'How did school go today?' she asked cheerily.

'Same as always, woman,' Bernard said, imitating his father.

'Anything unusual happen?'

'Like what?' tone implying how could anything unusual happen at school?

'Like the school burning down, you (something in Lithuanian),' Mrs. Milos screamed as she whacked at her truant son.

Chapter 29
Electrifying!

Campbell's was a store which opened just across the foot of Swan Street from Sadie Burns'. Mr. Campbell wasn't even, which was our way of saying he was odd. Maybe he was just Protestant.

The store was connected to their living quarters, and Mr. and Mrs. Campbell kept an aquarium in his living room. Not a tropical fish container, but he kept bullheads and catfish, edibles, in it. You could pick out one and he'd clean it and sell it to you.

What was more than unusual was his car, an old, dark blue Buick, which he had electrified. One of his pastimes was to sit in the car and when one of the many Woert Street dogs peed on it the electricity would follow up the urine stream -- and ...!

He and Mrs. Campbell, a heavy-set dowager, liked to drive down to the Gut in downtown Albany, sit in the security of their electrified safety, and watch the whores.

Campbell's store had a wide window on the Swan Street side. One early evening when we were in our early teens and upset with Sadie for something, we were hanging around Campbell's when a strange man outside started motioning to us. He kept pointing to us and then to his mouth. I didn't know who grasped his meaning first but we were astounded. This was out of our league, we all took off for my house and I went in to tell Daddy, who was nonchalant.

'Aren't you going do to something?' I asked.

He answered with a question of his own, 'How many of you are there?'

'Six,' I counted mentally.

'Then go tell him to get the hell out of the neighborhood' was Daddy's solution.

When we got back to the store, the man was gone forever.

It was then that somebody said, 'You know what? Maybe he only wanted something to eat.'

Chapter 30
Unforgettable

As part of my ninth birthday, July 31, 1941, Mother and Daddy let me go to the movies alone. I had money for candy and the Paramount. We were to have cake when I got back.

From Van Woert to the Paramount was only a mile or so, up Van Woert, shortcut alongside the Diamond to Lark, over to Clinton, right turn, crossing Northern Boulevard.

The show opened at 2. In those days, two features, the news, a cartoon, a serial, and coming attractions made for a full day. That day, the feature attraction was 'Meet John Doe' with Gary Cooper, Barbara Stanwyck, and Walter Brennan. It was preceded by a movie about a jockey. 'Meet John Doe' had a lot of baseball and underdog sympathy and righteousness, things of sheer joy for our Depression generation.

All by myself and comfortably ensconced with plenty of Milk Duds, I thoroughly got into my birthday treat. When I was leaving, Jerry Blanch and his mother Molly came in. I started telling Jerry how good the movie was. Then I decided to sit with Jerry to watch just a little more. Well, I sat through it all again -- the two movies, the news, the serial, cartoon and coming attractions.

When we got outside, it was beginning to turn dark -- in more ways than one. I took off running. On Van Woert, the people were already summer-sitting on their stoops.

'Your father has been looking for you!'

'Boy, are you going to get it when you get home!'

Phrases I heard many times as life bounced along on Van Woert Street.

Soon I could see Daddy standing outside the empty lot next to our house. Suspenders, arm bands, arms folded across his chest, typical Jinx. When I got there, he surprised me with a quiet question:

'What is today's date?'

Maybe things weren't so bad, after all.

'July 31st,' I said, walking a little wide of Daddy as we entered the yard.

'Wait,' he said, 'what year?'

'1941.' I could sense something different, something dire.

'And why is it special for you ?' he said, smiling, the last rays of the sun bouncing off his gold tooth.

'It's my birthday.'

'Which one?' he pressed on.

'My ninth.'

'Well,' he said, swinging into action, 'I'm going to give you something so you'll never forget your ninth birthday as long as you live.'

He turned out to be right.

Swinging wildly, he chased me upstairs where I was to stay. When flying through the kitchen, I noticed my living-saint Aunt Margaret had come for the party. I couldn't believe I would have to stay upstairs while they were eating my birthday cake. After a while, Margaret came upstairs with cake and ice cream. Handing them to me, she said, 'You know your father's right, don't you?'

'Yes.'

She gave me a hug, said 'happy birthday' and handed me a present from somebody. It was a Big Little Book, Dick Tracy.

Well, this is as good a place as any to give the Paramount Theater a little ink. What? You could do it better? Go ahead, try! But the memoirist gets to be boss. That's the way it works.

The best thing about the Paramount was that it cost only a dime on Saturday; the next best thing was the person who ran it who was known to the kids as Bessie the Bull! She not only kept under control some hundred youngsters full of poppin' Milk Duds but ran the distribution of free china pieces to war-weary parents at evening movies.

It was relatively easy to sneak into the downtown movie houses, except for young Frankie Cardamone who, for the thrill of it, used to crawl along the catwalk atop the Palace Theater' stage paraphernalia to get in from an outside exit high over North Pearl Street.

Free entry into the Paramount was relatively simple-- open any door leading in from the Clinton Avenue was all --- if it weren't for Bessie the Bull who was a 'one-man' commando force, tall and bulky, a shifty runner with a capable 'OSS' force to catch and report any break-ins. Indeed, there was more than 'Coop' in the Saturday cast; thanks to Bessie.

Chapter 31
Missing Sister Alice

For a while after the SJA fire, we were out of school; then we began taking classes at the convent on North Pearl Street which wasn't big enough for all of us so we would go maybe a half-day or two a week. The ambiance of the Sisters' home wasn't conducive to learning and the perfume from the bread baking at the National Biscuit Company next door was a monstrous, though pleasurable, distraction.

Eventually, we had to find new schools. On Jan. 17, 1945, Neile F. Towner, president of the public school board of education, offered to permit either part or the entire group of SJA children into the public school system. Bernard and I took him up on it and opted for Philip Livingston Junior High School; I can't remember our parents objecting.

'Cousin' Frankie Cardamone, catcher nonpareil from Colonie Street, and others

went to Holy Cross School in the South
End.

'The Sisters are really nice,' Frankie
reported on his new surroundings.

'Nothing like St. Joseph's. But,' he said,
grimacing, 'they are not too bright.'

He said a couple of the guys were horsing
around in class with a 'cundrum' (what we
called condoms) when the sister spotted
them and made them turn it over to her.

'She took it back to her desk,' Frankie said.
'She looked it over for a while and finally
asked the kid what it was for. We were all
giggling. I spoke up, 'It's for turning pages
... you put it on your thumb.'

'She began to use it that way ' would you
believe it' But after lunch she didn't have
it any more.'

Frankie's parents were immigrants.
Summer nights, his father would sit on
their Colonie Street front stoop and play
the mandolin. He and Mrs. Cardamone
spoke pidgin English.

One day after school, Frankie asked his
mother what was for supper.

'Pasta fazool,' she said.

'Oh no,' Frankie remonstrated, 'Not again.
I hate pasta fazool.'

Mrs. Cardamone turned calmly to me and smilingly asked, 'You like-a pasta fazool?' 'Yes,' I answered honestly. At which Mrs. Cardamone smacked Frankie, 'See, Carmen likea pasta fazool and he's-a half Americano.'

Some time in January 1945, I arrived at Philip Livingston. Differences abounded -- the first being the cafeteria. The smell of food in school was so striking that to this day I am transported back to Livingston whenever I get a whiff of institutional cooking.

Another adjustment -- gym. Father Looney disapproved of it; he didn't like the idea of young people undressing together, even though St. Joseph's did have a high school basketball program, producing some excellent teams.

So in the seventh grade, I had gym for the first time and found out that I could run pretty fast. In the citywide track meet I scored 13 points (won the 50-yard dash, was on the winning relay team, and was second in the broad jump in my group; we were divided based on strength).

The Times-Union had a story the next day. There was my name -- 'Charles Viglucci.'

Oh, well.

Also different was what seemed to me an amazing lack of discipline. Kids flaunted the authority of teachers -- not all kids; not all teachers.

At the end of one day, a substitute teacher, rattled by unruly students, moaned, 'Please, please, give me something bright to look back on.'

'Turn around and look out the window,' came a merciless reply.

Egad, was I getting nostalgic for Sister Alice?

Because of the St. Joseph's background, for a while I was far in advance of the others, particularly in English and math. Could it be that the Sisters of Charity knew what they were doing?

Chapter 32
Decolletage at 14

At the beginning of each school year, we all had to take physicals. In the eighth grade, it was discovered that I had a heart murmur -- no gym, no track.

Someone suggested I go to my family doctor and Mother took me to Dr. Heim who said he didn't think the murmur was serious enough to alter my activities. But, in any case, I had to wait until next year's physical.

In Albany at that time, some of the public schools were K-8 and thus in the ninth grade a whole bunch of new students arrived at Philip Livingston. As I was carrying some new books down the aisle, I tripped over someone's foot, no accident, and I nearly fell, dropping the books. I bent to pick them up when the same toe nudged them farther away. I looked down sharply and there was this beaming girl with eyes that only can be described tritely as piercing, light brown hair with bangs, and, believe it or not, a low-cut blouse. In the ninth grade!

Jane Russ was from Oklahoma City, lived in North Albany now, and would occupy a lot of my thoughts for some time.

That fall, some kids had scheduled a hayride and I decided to go. I had no idea what a hayride was but was going to ask Jane Russ to go. We didn't have a telephone at home, so I set out to choose a public booth. None on Arbor Hill seemed to be just right, and I ended up all the way downstreet.

Trodding along North Pearl, I made a mental register of all the available booths as I rehearsed my speech over and over. I refined the approach to a smithereen over a couple of hours of traipsing up and down past the stores.

It was beginning to get dark when I finally went into a drugstore near Clinton Square and dialed her number -- 5-7698.

'Hello,' it was she.

'Hi, this is Carmen ...' Silence. I persisted, 'Carmen ... Viglucci ... from school'' I was getting ready to run off.

'I know,' her tone suggesting 'of course.' 'Did you do your homework yet?'

'Yes.'

I was out of small talk.

'You wouldn't want to go on that hayride with me, would you?' -- slick, huh'

'Sure.'

There it was ... 20 seconds ... all it took to date the best-looking girl at Philip Livingston. The next day, I acted nonchalant when I informed my friend Santo Buongiorno. Should my feelings have been hurt when he didn't believe me'

Along about then came my ninth grade physical. I was called out of Miss Holdahl's Science Class. We used tables for desks in science and Santo and I shared one, just behind Jane and another student.

The school doctor said the murmur was still there and ... too bad.

When I returned to class, I told Santo. When Jane turned around, inquisitively, I merely shook my head no. To my surprise, she began to tear up. Right there. In class. I, for once, was at a loss for words.

Chapter 33
Class Struggle

Livingston was really a polyglot. It was the public junior high for the entire north segment of the city -- kids from the poor neighborhoods, blacks from Arbor Hill, middle class types from the western part of the city, and some well-off kids from Loudonville and environs.

A group of the latter belonged to a football team called the Menands Red Raiders. They played six-man, wore uniforms and equipment, and talked a good game. Santo and I, the original classists, decided to challenge them to a game and were stunned when they accepted. We had to get a team together in a hurry. We managed to get Bob Basch, Sanford Cohen, Sam Milham and Tommy Hall to join us -- then there were six -- two Italians, a Jew, an Arab, and a Protestant (Tommy's father was sexton at the famed First Church of Albany) -- taking on the rich Goliaths. Let me be quick to add that over time were to learn that at least two members of the Red Raiders were all-right guys -- Ed Van Akin and James Bennett. About our guys: Bob Basch was on the short side but had a good build; Sanford Cohen suffered 'the agony of psoriasis, but was bulky; Sam Milham was tallish and thinnish; Tommy Hall was a church sexton's son; Santo Bongiorno had wavy dark hair and a flashy grin; and I weighed in at about 120. None of us had ever played in an organized football game. Thus on a Saturday morning at the famous Bleecker Stadium, we managed to get in an hour of practice, during which we couldn't agree on a name for our team. Then about 20 Menands Red Raiders showed up -- on a bus no less, with uniformed officials, parents, and Jane Russ on board. She was friends with one of the Menands players from Milne High School. And there we were, six, in our mismatched sweatshirts and Levis and sneakers.

We won the coin flip, elected to receive, I caught the kickoff, lateraled off to Santo and he ran all the way for a touchdown. We had six -- and that was all we were to get. We lost, 20-6.

After the game, Sam Milham hoped his loosened tooth wouldn't come out; Sanford Cohen threw up; Santo hopped around, grimacing; Tommy left in a hurry, and I lay wretching in the end zone. I sensed someone standing there.

I squinted up, blocking the noon sun to see.

'You all right?' Jane Russ asked.

'Don't miss your bus,' I answered.

Chapter 34
Principal of the Thing

Most of the kids at Livingston saw our principal, Mr. Edward Devey, as a mean old cuss (they didn't know the Sisters of Charity). He took a liking to me and chose me for a photo in the Times Union raising the school's safety banner on the front lawn.

Then Dr. IQ, a national radio personality, put on his show at Livingston and Mr. Devey arranged for me to be a contestant. I missed an easy one -- 'What track and field event couldn't be held in a prison?' My reply: the mile run; the answer was the pole vault.

But when I answered 'a hole' to the question 'What's nothing with something around it?' I won the show and a wristwatch.

Then in the ninth grade, when the Albany Symphony performed one night at the school and they needed ushers, Mr. Devey volunteered me, David Skoglund, a paperboy friend who would die shortly thereafter from leukemia; Jane Russ (were we becoming Mickey Rooney and Judy Garland?) and, among others, Carl DeFlumer, who happened to be a friend of Bernard's.

It was a typical Albany winter night and, after the concert, as the audience left, Carl lobbed snowballs, impregnated with stones, into the departing crowd. The rest of us tried to dissuade him '- but he was having too much fun. Some adult got upset and chased after him but a giggling Carl got away.

After I was graduated from Livingston, Mr. Devey was the center of a story concerning my friend Puggy LaMountain from Van Woert Street. Puggy, who in the ninth grade drove to school himself, had poured sand into the gas tank of Mr. Devey's car and in response the principal called a general assembly of students.

'What would happen,' Mr. Devey asked, 'if a student got ill or hurt and I carried him to my car to take him to emergency, and because some cur fouled up my gas, my car wouldn't start?'

His audience had barely time to soak in the question when the indomitable Puggy shouted out, 'I'd take him!'

It was a giveaway and Puggy was in hot water, to the point of suspension.

One day, to my surprise, Mr. Devey and his wife came into the State News as customers. They seemed just a kindly older couple. Still, I didn't mention Puggy in our brief conversation.

Chapter 35
Hard Times

While on the subject of Puggy LaMountain--we worked out a little routine. If there was a group of people waiting at a bus stop and it included a woman, say, 45 or 50, we would move in. When the bus arrived, one of us would start to get on and the other would say, 'Wait a minute, let the old lady on first.' We spread joy and goodwill everywhere we went.

Puggy had two older brothers, Junie and Tar Baby, and a younger sister, Jeanette, who was good friends with sister Honey. At first, they lived over the Tiger AC but later moved farther down on the other side of the street, near the Coxes.

When Junie was about 16 he was arrested in connection with a burglary. It was reported in the paper that he confessed. He was let out on bail and told us the police forced his confession. We had reason to believe him -- his face was lumpy and black-and-blue enough to give credence to his story.

He was not the only Van Woert Streeter to run afoul of the law. Arnold Villeneuve, the oldest child in a family who lived next to the soda factory (was it Par-T-Pak or Nehi?) -- served a sentence at Dannemora. Upon completion, he was reveling in his freedom, sitting on his front stoop with his younger brothers Billy and Kenny and sister Loretta along with Bernard and Kenny Wright, whose family lived on the top floor over the Villeneuves.

'Finian's Rainbow' was popular at the time and arriving amid this auspicious gathering, I couldn't resist singing to Arnold, 'How are things in Dannemora?' The quick punch that decked me indicated that he probably hadn't seen 'Finian's Rainbow.'

After Bernard and I started going to Livingston, and didn't have to face the Sisters any more, we began to skip Mass more than we went.

We each would be given two quarters, one for the collection, the other to get the Sunday Times-Union. We would divert

'one two-bits' (Spencer Tracy in 'Tortilla Flat') from God to Caesar and buy ice cream sodas at Mr. Hayes', next to V. J. Franze's big grocery store near SJA, and a block and a half from the church. If I got strawberry, Bernard would get chocolate -- or vice versa. While downing the soda we would read the sports pages. Then when the 10:15 Mass got out we would collar someone on the way home:
'Who said the sermon today? What was it about?'
We had to be ready when and if our mothers quizzed us, which mine often did and I'll bet Big Bertha (she's not around, is she?) did.

One such Sunday at the soda fountain, when we took the news sections out from the funnies wrapper we were stunned to read this 72 point double decker:
**'Playmate Seized in Death
Of Boy, 8, Near Shaker Road,'**

Subheads read 'Child Found Hanging Nude from Tree with Hands Tied,' and then 'Robert Wahrman Is Victim, Suspect

Faces Charge of Murder.'
The story said:
'A first degree murder charge will be placed this morning against Carl DeFlumer in the slaying of eight-year-old Robert Wahrman, according to District Attorney Julian B. Erway.'
Carl had gone a long way from pelting concert-goers with snowballs.
'DeFlumer,' the story continued, 'confessed readily to hanging the boy in a patch of woods near Shaker Road, Loudonville, the District Attorney announced just before midnight last night. He had been brought in a general roundup of boys in the neighborhood.
'He quoted Deflumer as saying he was the only participant and that he and Robert were walking through the woods together when the thought occurred to him of hanging him.
'DeFlumer said he had been carrying a rope with him all morning 'for tying up papers' and he slipped it around the other lad's neck.
'...Mr. Erway described the DeFlumer boy as being quite husky for his age but not of a tough type. In fact, he was quite calm

and self-possessed in making the confession.'

The story was obviously a new lead on an earlier edition story and a different person seemed to have written it than the one who did the pickup which was an example of the worst kind of Hearst journalism. The Times-Union either sloppily or deliberately left in details of the earlier story, quoting a priest: 'How an adult could do a thing like this I do not know.'

It included a subhead, 'Hunt Maniac Clues' and such sensational language as, 'Bobby was found in almost supine position. Neither the District Attorney nor police would give any indication of the kind of fiend they believed committed so hideous a crime, but it was understood there was the possibility that a sex maniac might have been involved.'

The paper audaciously printed a Page 1 photo of the coroner in the gray fedora of the time examining 'the body of eight-year-old Robert Wahrman found hanged yesterday ...' showing the dead boy's body. As the drama played out, the district attorney said the murder was an 'impulse crime' and that there was no other injury other that caused by the rope. There was no sexual molestation.

Carl DeFlumer spent the next 20 years of his life in prison.

That Sunday morning, there was a lot more to digest than strawberry ice cream and the Albany Senators.

Penance

'Bless me, Father, for I have sinned ... it's been two months since my last confession. I have missed Mass seven times. I ...'

'Wait a minute, son. It's only been two months since you confessed and you've missed Mass how many times?'

'Seven, Father.'

Silence.

'What does your mother say?'

'She doesn't know. I mean she thinks I went.'

'Doesn't this involve lying?'

'Kind of.'

'Well, for your Penance, five Hail Marys and five Our Fathers ...'

'Whew,' I thought to myself, 'not so bad.'

'... And you must tell your mother you lied

to her.'
And to think I chose this confessional
because he was a visiting priest.
He was asking too much. He didn't know
my mother. I couldn't tell her ... so I didn't
go to confession again for 15 years.

Chapter 36
Show Business

It's a good thing the Andy Hardy movies came first or else we could have accused Hollywood of plagiarizing. Every summer in the '40s we would put on a show for the neighborhood.

Cousin Joan Waters who lived next door at 94 Van Woert was generally the producer and director, and she and sister Honey, and assorted Rhatigans mostly sang and danced or showed off hats; Bernard and I and maybe Puggy LaMountain and Billy Villeneuve would put on boxing matches, but the undisputed star was Jerry Blanch who could play the trumpet. When he blew 'I've Heard That Song Before,' it was easy to close your eyes and picture Harry James himself.

I think we charged ten cents admission but for those who couldn't come up with the dough we would accept soda bottles (2 cents deposit) or cookies or such to be sold at the show. Afterward the performers would split the take evenly, though Jerry, and maybe Joan, deserved a higher percentage.

Chapter 37
Prince of a Boss

And so on to Albany High School where I would meet Tony Tartaglia, Fred Weber and Howie Serling, who would become life long friends.

One summer break, I worked for Howie's grandfather, Mr. Katz, at the Jewish cemeteries on Western Avenue and Fuller Road.

Being a Gentile working at a Jewish cemetery was not nearly as difficult as the routine of getting up in the pre-dawn hours, taking the Beltline bus downtown, transferring to Western Avenue and going to the end of the line to wait for Mr. Katz's blue pickup truck to take me the rest of the way.

It was a most eventful summer for me mainly because of the Jewish tradition wherein folks who die early enough in the day are buried before sundown. This meant that often I would have to work unexpectedly late in the afternoon.

And would you believe that on my very

first day on the job we had to inter an Albany High classmate who was killed in an auto crash the night before, kind of a rough way to begin.

Then in a few days, another classmate's mother died and that was another sad chore. We had to shovel dirt on the pine boxes. Each time, a shovelful thumped, it drew loud wails from the assemblage.

But as should be expected, life at the cemetery was not without its humor. On one such burial, I, in my Colonie Indian baseball cap, and Mr. Katz, in his sweat-stained brown fedora, were standing side by side as the cantor sang. I noticed Mr. Katz shaking some and when I looked, I saw he was chuckling.

He thrust the death certificate at me and whispered, 'See what he died from.'

My nervous eyes made out 'elephantiasis' which still meant nothing to me.

'Elephantiasis,' Mr. Katz hissed, 'big potatas!'

Howie's and my duties at the cemetery consisted mainly of cutting grass and filling in graves. Digging the hole required a certain expertise and Mr. Katz had a couple of expert gravediggers who could do a sharply-sided grave post haste.

One perfect June day as I was cutting grass, my mind turned to thoughts of Joe D, Tommy Henrich, Gene Woodling, et al, when my reverie was interrupted by Mr. Katz calling, 'Come over, we need your help.'

When I got where the three of them were standing together, I noticed they had dug up a grave and had straps under a dirt-covered, caved-in box. The four of us managed to pull it up and place it next to a shipping vault and I went back to Gene Woodling.

A short time later, Mr. Katz called: 'We need you again.'

'You get where you were before,' he said, meaning the head of the box. When I leaned down, I found myself staring into the sunken eyes of a female corpse, whose shroud was riddled with insect holes and wettened to stick to the face.

I instinctively jerked my head away.

Mr. Katz said, 'Don't worry, she won't bite.'

The reason for the disinterment was that the lady was to be shipped to Israel for permanent burial.

One night, I did a little night-life-ing with my friends Bob Sweeney and Tom Ryan. We drank beer until quite late and the next morning I called and told Mrs. Katz I had gotten food poisoning at a Chinese food restaurant the previous night and couldn't make it to work. She commiserated and all was well. I was Scot-free, I thought.

I should point out that Mr. Katz was one of the best bosses I've ever had -- anywhere. He took his duties very seriously and I always thought his results were excellent. He also managed to inject some humor into what could be a very somber and stressful business, without overdoing it which could be sacrilegious in some cases. Sometimes on days when there were no burials and it was particularly hot, after work, Mr. Katz would take us all to a bar on Western Avenue -- Howie, the gravediggers, and myself. About two weeks after my bogus telephone call, we all stopped at the bar. As I was taking a long quaff of the cold beer. Mr. Katz with a twinkle in his eye asked, 'How's the Chinese food here?'

Chapter 38
Loudonville Yeshiva

The time came when educational choices had to be made. Andrew was the first person among the two family branches to go to college -- Clark University in Worcester, Mass. He did so with aid of the GI Bill.

The assumption was that I also would seek higher education. Fine, but how? I had actually saved a thousand dollars or so but had no idea of the economics or logistics of college-going much less a particular higher hall of learning in store for me.

I had heard that Boston University was pretty good in journalism and I also was interested in Alabama, because I liked the name Tuscaloosa. Honest!

Being a teacher had some appeal. I at least knew where the State Teachers College was -- right next door to Albany High School. And tuition at state colleges was very affordable.

Our principal, Dr. Harry S. Pratt, was no Mr. Devey, so when he invited me into his office it was the only time I ever talked to him, though we were both involved in the business of my education for three years under the same roof. I was nervous; I could tell Dr. Pratt wasn't. I knew instinctively he knew a lot more about me than I about him. Ditto the agenda.

He leaned back in his swivel chair, thumbs tucked into the vest part of his three-part gray flannel suit. The image popped into my mind of Sister Mary and Mother.

He swiveled in and out of my line of vision and asked why I wanted to be a teacher -- for which I had no glib reason. I had an average of about 88, not too bad, considering a 45 in Solid Geometry.

'I see,' Dr. Pratt said, scanning my transcript, pretending he hadn't looked at it before. 'You had 98 in Algebra and then 45 in Solid Geometry. How do you explain that"

'Miss Seelman (Algebra) is a great teacher.'

'So when you started to slide in Solid Geometry, what did you do?'

Who ever wanted to be a teacher anyway?

'I let 'er slide,' I answered, more truthfully than I realized.

Dr. Pratt chuckled a little then after a carefully-planned thoughtful pause, cleared his throat, and said, 'I don't think I can recommend you for State Teachers College.'

End of interview; abortion of possible teaching career.

I had also applied to Siena College, a Franciscan college in the suburb of Loudonville, founded only a dozen years previously and called among other things, Loudonville Yeshiva, because so many Jewish kids went there. But I was beginning to realize that the near-thousand dollars I had saved would not go far especially with the dismal weakness Dr. Pratt had exposed.

Fate took a hand. Siena invited all Albany area applicants to take a scholarship test. As destiny dictated, it was a multiple choice examination. If you only relied on guessing, you would get 25 percent correct on the four options.

The test seemed easy but long -- still I was a little worried when I finished and waited and waited ... and waited ... for someone else to do the same.

'Maybe I missed a page,' I worried. No.

When I handed it in the brown-robed monitor looked at me strangely. That was that.

Imagine my surprise a couple of weeks later when I received a letter; I had won the scholarship, worth half-tuition for four years. I was headed for Loudonville Yeshiva--where I would meet Herb Smith of Warrensburg, who would become another life-long friend.

Chapter 39
Scholarship
Saves the Day!

Before, when I was beginning to doubt that college was in my future, I had worried some about telling Daddy, who had hounded me since diapers about going to college. That day, he was the first to know; I showed him the letter when I arrived for work at the State News. More than a hint of tears showed in his eyes and he patted me on the back. He was pleased. So was I.

Shortly after, Fred Weber from Madison Avenue and I spent two glorious weeks, July 9 to 23, at the Great Lakes Naval Training Station near Chicago, as part of our Navy Reserve duty. I got home on a Saturday and was listening to two of my favorite 45s -- 'Mona Lisa' by Nat Cole and 'Rhapsody in Blue,' by the Paul Whiteman Orchestra.

During the latter, Daddy sat down and listened for a while. 'You like classical music?'

'Kind of.'

'How about Duke Ellington?'

'Yeah ...' I said, not too aware of anything but 'Mood Indigo.'

'Who's to say Duke Ellington isn't classical?'

I started to realize that Daddy had something on his mind and it wasn't 'Sophisticated Lady.' But he didn't get to it that day.

When I got home from work a few nights later, there was Daddy sitting in his A-type undershirt at the kitchen table ... sober.

Something was up.

'Sit down,' he more motioned than said.

'Remember how we talked about opening up another place on Broadway?'

Daddy and Steve had mentioned a second newsroom, part diner, to be called The Whistlestop, across from the train station on Broadway.

'Well, we're going to do it.'

'Yeah?' I questioned carefully.

'And I want you to manage it.'

I tried to bundle this idea mentally but it wouldn't gather.

'But I'll be going to school.'

'Well, that's what we have to talk about.'

He was reading my eyes.

'I have a proposition for you. If you forget about college and take over the Whistlestop, we'll pay you a good salary plus I'll buy you a roadster.'

A long pause. I looked him in the eye.

'What's a roadster?'

Daddy shook his head carefully, I could hear him thinking, 'Jesus, you don't know what a roadster is? A fancy car.'

'I don't know ...'

'That's all right,' he said. 'Take a few days. Think about it. Whatever you decide is okay.'

I started to get up but he held his hand out -- 'One more thing. Don't tell your mother about this conversation. If you decide to do it -- it's all your idea. Understand'?

Carmine Antonio Vigliucci didn't say 'capisce' as Jack Devine would.

'Yeah,' I did understand.

It was a decision I never had to make.

Chapter 40
The King Himself
Scores with Kid

Earlier I referenced that among my best bosses of all time was Mr. Katz at the Jewish Cemeteries. Another was Jack Andrews many years later at the sports desk of the Syracuse (NY) Post-Standard. He wasn't the sports editor but somehow, I, a neophyte, became his protégé--maybe because he also was an Albanian, or because my early job portfolio included the position of paperboy. I delivered the Knick News but years before Jack delivered the morning Times Union. That meant he was a morning paperboy in the South End which meant he had to get up early to make deliveries. When finished he usually took a nap.

One particular Saturday morn he asked his mother to be extra sure to wake him at 10 sharp because it was a big day. Babe Ruth was coming to town for a batting exhibition.

Now, if there were only person in all Capital District, unaware of this event, it would have to be Jack's mom. She let Jack sleep.

The boy no longer could be on time for the show.

But he tried. Clutching his newly bought baseball, he ran, and ran, and ran -- but you get the idea. Sweating, he came to the juncture where North Pearl straightened into Broadway. Leaning and squinting from there, Jack could see a big car leaving a crowd in front of Hawkins Stadium. As the limo rolled down Broadway toward the Holy City, Jack crouched to get a sight of its occupant but failed to do so as the big car passed but miracle of miracles, it stopped and backed slowly to him. The back window slid down;

'Whatcha got there, kid?' Jack will never forget that voice. 'Give it here,' a huge hand waggled to him. Quickly, every American's boy's icon affixed that clear signature, handed it over then flashed a good-luck thumbs-up, as the moment wended into eternity.

Epilogue

It is safe to say, that if the Fitzgeralds knew their actual genealogy, there would have been no cause for any Irish-Italian differences. The national bloodlines of the two families are much closer than they ever would have believed.

This writer, too, only recently became aware of this fact and had trouble accepting it, though it has been public knowledge for centuries.

Instead of immediately producing the historical proof, first let me explain how it came to me. During the year 2005 I helped produce a series called 'Italnet' on a television channel in Rochester, New York. Each show consisted of a travelogue of Italy, Italian music clips, poetry by the station's owner Gianni Catalano, and local Italian news. I was responsible for two segments, an 'editorial' and interviews with local luminaries.

One day, I interviewed a widely known and respected local 'avvocato,' Franklin D'Aurizio. We were chatting after the official interview and I told him I was half-Irish and that mother's mother's name was Fitzgerald. He chuckled and asked, 'Did you know JFK had Italian roots?' Though I instinctively knew D'Aurizio was above mundane jokes, I still cringed a little wondering if he had some off-color humor in mind.

As I should have known, he was serious. About a week later, D'Aurizio mailed me a copy of the February-March 2003 edition of American Italian Heritage Digest, published in, of all places, Albany, New York. Highlighted on Page 8 was this item: *'Was there a president with Italian 'roots?' If you said yes, you were correct. John F. Kennedy's maternal grandfather's name was Fitzgerald and they were descended from the Geraldinis who supposedly came from Venice. When they went to Ireland, they changed their name to Fitzgerald. JFK, on a speech on Columbus Day in New Jersey, disclosed he had Italian 'roots,' the press checked it out and confirmed it.'* Further lending credence was this Oct. 19, 1962 news item from Time.com 'J.F.K. on the Stump ' The next morning Kennedy popped over to attend a Columbus Day celebration, revealed to a heavily Italian crowd of 10,000 ,a campaign trick of his grandfather's, Boston's John F. ('Honey Fitz') Fitzgerald.

Kennedy said, 'My grandfather always used to claim that the Fitzgeralds were descended from the Geraldinis, who came from Venice. I have never had the courage to make that claim, but I will make it on Columbus Day in this state of New Jersey.''

You, dear reader, as I did, may have doubts about this. Suspect a political strategy on JFK's part, or his grandfather's? Or just a plain mistake? If so, do as the redoubtable Casey Stengle of the world of baseball would advise, 'Look it up!'

I did just that --on Google. I entered 'The Geraldini and the Fitzgeralds.'

Under a large headline 'Geraldini' was the underline 'la famiglia Geraldine.'

Then the following:

'FitzGerald (Geraldini of Florence). Sir Maurice Fitz Gerald(a) First Baron of Offaly; born about 1152 in Florence, died before 15 Jan 1203/04. He married Eve de Bermingham about 1185, the daughter of Robert de Bermingham.

'Their child was Sir Maurice FitzGerald, justiciar of Ireland, Lord of Offaly, Knight / born 1190, died 1257.'

Please notice that county 'Offaly which family historian Dennis Fitzgerald (mentioned in this book) ascertained was the birthplace of our own Fitzgerald family. *A John Kearney of the Offaly Historical Society,* wrote Dennis, *recorded that 'fifty-six persons left Kilconcourse (the crown estate situated in the parish of Kinnity, King's County).'* Offaly was also known as King's County.

'Fifty-six left Kilconcourse 11 June 1852 ' on the list Fitzgerald John 42 years, Ellen, wife 30, Denis, son 12, Thomas, son 8 and Margaret, daughter 10 ' I then turned to the Kinnity parish baptism and marriage records ' John Fitzgerald of Kyle (townland) and Ellen Spain got married on 14 February 1841.'

Diligent Dennis then accurately places John Fitzgerald and Ellen Spain on the present-day family tree with Timothy E. Fitzgerald, 1878-1960, the modern patriarch.

But, you may interject, Kennedy said 'Venice.' Just a minor mistake, born of covering a millennium. Likely a member of the Geraldini family was a Venetian. In any case, there is further evidence of the Ireland-Florence, Tuscany tie. More from the internet, this time under Geraldini.com:*The early Bendings were members of the Norman family, the Windsors, descendants of the Gherardini (editor's note: family name; Geraldini was Latin translation). The first of these to come to England was Dominus Other, who was present at the court of Edward the Confessor, from about 1056. This man through his son, Walter, was the founder of the Windsor and the Fitzgerald families.* Here's some historical poetry from the Bendings:

In the land of Hetruria there flourished once a
Mighty vine thither translated from the desolate
Plains of Troy. Florence claimed this beauteous
Plant her own; and well might she glory in it, for
'its branches stretched forth unto the sea, and its
Boughs into the river.' From the banks

of the
Arno and the shores of the blue
Tyrrhene Sea the
Branches of the great tree extend
themselves to
The far land of Erin. The great tree was
the noble
race of the Geraldines, who, under the
shadow of
Tuscan banners, penetrated regions
whither
Roman legions never dare to venture.'

Hetruria signifies the mysterious race that once settled in central Italy ' the Etruscans, whose coming and going have never been historically decided. Seems that the Bendings believed that the Etruscans and Geraldinis, that is the Fitzgeralds, were one.
Note also that the Geraldinis, that is the Fitzgeralds, and the ancient land of Troy have been linked. From Troy. of ancient Asia Minor to Troy, of New York. Fun, isn't it?
Here's how a more modern Irish poet, Thomas Osborne Davis himself (1814-1845), connects the Fitzes, Tuscany, and

Ireland:

*The Geraldines! The Geraldines!—'tis full a
thousand years Since, 'mid the Tuscan
vineyards, bright flashed their battle-
spears; When Capet seized the crown of
France, their iron shields were known, And
their sabre-dint struck terror on the banks
of the Garonne: Across the downs of
Hastings they spurred hard by William's
side, And the grey sands of Palestine with
Moslem blood they dyed; But never then,
nor thence till now, has falsehood or
disgrace Been seen to soil Fitzgerald's
plume, or mantle in his face.*

*The Geraldines! The Geraldines!—'tis true,
in Strongbow's van, By lawless force, as
conquerors, their Irish reign began; And,
oh! through many a dark campaign they
proved their prowess stern, In Leinster's
plains, and Munster's vales, on king, and
chief, and kerne; But noble was the cheer
within the halls so rudely won, And
generous was the steel-gloved hand that*

had such slaughter done; How gay their laugh, how proud their mien, you'd ask no herald's sign— Among a thousand you had known the princely Geraldine.
These Geraldines! These Geraldines!—not long our air they breathed; Not long they fed on venison, in Irish water seethed; Not often had their children been by Irish mothers nursed; When from their full and genial hearts an Irish feeling burst! The English monarchs strove in vain, by law, and force, and bribe, To win from Irish thoughts and ways this 'more than Irish' tribe; For still they clung to fosterage, to **breitheamh**, cloak, and bard: What king dare say to Geraldine, 'Your Irish wife discard'?

Ye Geraldines! ye Geraldines!—How royally ye reigned O'er Desmond broad and rich Kildare, and English arts disdained: Your sword made knights, your banner waved, free was your bugle call By Gleann's green slopes, and Daingean's tide, from Bearbha's banks to Eochaill. What gorgeous shrines, what **breitheamh** lore, what minstrel feasts there were In and around Magh Nuadhaid's keep, and palace-filled Adare! But not for rite or feast ye stayed, when friend or kin were pressed; And foeman fled when 'Crom-abu' bespoke your lance in rest.

Ye Geraldines! ye Geraldines!—since Silken Thomas flung King Henry's sword on council board, the English thanes among,

Ye never ceased to battle brave against the English sway, Though axe and brand and treachery your proudest cut away. Of Desmond's blood through woman's veins passed on th' exhausted tide; His title lives—a **Sacsanach** churl usurps the lion's hide; And though Kildare tower haughtily, there's ruin at the root, Else why, since Edward fell to earth, had such a tree no fruit?

True Geraldines! Brave Geraldines!—as torrents mould the earth, You channeled deep old Ireland's heart by constancy and worth: When Ginckle 'leaguered Limerick, the Irish soldiers gazedTo see if the setting sun dead Desmond's banner blazed! And *still it is the peasant's hope upon the Cuirreach's mere, 'They live, who'll see ten thousand men with good Lord Edward here.'— So let them dream till brighter days, when, not by Edward's shade, But by some leader true as he, their lines shall be arrayed!*

These Geraldines! These Geraldines!—rain wears away the rock And time may wear away the tribe that stood the battle's shock; But ever, sure, while one is left of all that honoured race,

In front of Ireland's chivalry is that Fitzgerald's place: And though the last were dead and gone, how many a field and town, From Thomas Court to Abbeyfeile, would cherish their renown! And men will say of valour's rise, or ancient power's decline, "T will never soar, it never shone, as did the Geraldine.'

The Geraldines! the Geraldines!—and are there any fears Within the sons of conquerors for full a thousand years? Can treason spring from out a soil bedewed with martyr's blood? Or has that grown a purling brook which long rushed down a flood?— By Desmond swept with sword and fire—by clan and keep laid low— By Silken Thomas and his kin,—by sainted Edward! No! The forms of centuries rise up, and in the Irish line Command their son to take the post that fits the Geraldine!

And wouldn't Aunt Anne be surprised? But no longer chagrined!

The End

CJV

Carmen Viglucci's career in the newspaper business began when he was 12 and became a news carrier for The Knickerbocker News. Following a stint in the Army's news information office during the Korean War, he attended Siena College working on the sports section of the college newspaper. Upon graduation, he got a call from The Albany Times-Union and was soon on the staff of that paper's sports desk. From there it was to a similar position on the Syracuse Post Standard which eventually brought him to the Rochester Democrat and Chronicle as a copy editor and night city editor. Later he became editor of the Rochester diocesan newspaper, The Catholic Courier Journal. In 1976 he founded a newspaper for seniors, The Golden Times where he and son John Viglucci worked together for 20 years.

Newspaper ink runs in the Viglucci family's veins. Viglucci's father Carmen (Jinx) was a circulation manager of the Knickerbocker News (before his son's carrier days) and his brother Andy (with fellow Albanian William Kennedy) founded The San Juan Star in Puerto Rico in the 1950s. Later when Andy returned to his roots, he became Managing Editor of The Albany Times Union. Andy's son Andres Viglucci continues the family tradition as a reporter for The

Miami Herald. Carmen welcomes

comments, additional information and suggestions. Contact him by email: cjviglucci@gmail.com. If you enjoyed this book, please pass the word along.

Now enjoy an excerpt from "Growing Up Italian in God's Country: Stories From the Wilds of Pennsylvania," by Patricia Costa Viglucci.

GOING TO CONRAD-1941

The excitement begins to grow even before I awake. Something delicious is happening today. Eyes still closed, I stretch carefully so as not to wake my little sister Thomasina. Spring air off the newly green hills balloons white, filmy curtains. The one sparkling window in the tiny room faces east. No hint that the Bayless paper mill with its smokestacks and lumberyard lies just around the bend, the great broken slabs of its concrete dam a few miles north.

Cotton sheets, crisp and sweet-smelling from being dried outside, further attest to my young mother's housekeeping abilities. Short-sleeved pajamas have replaced the winter flannels and the cool air on bare arms sends me snuggling back under the covers. In a flash I remember. It is Saturday. We are going to Conrad!

The trip from our home in Austin. to Mom's girlhood home is one we make nearly every week depending on the state of the dirt roads. A sea of mud in early spring or waist-high snow in the dead of winter might stop us but not much else. The long wait until 9 p.m. when Dad closes Gilroy's Grocery on Main Street makes going to see Grandma and Grandpa Borelli and my young aunts and uncle that much sweeter.

Conrad, also known as Hull or Hulls, in the East Fork district of Potter County, is 18 miles east , and arguably the wildest part of Pennsylvania. Mom was born there and grew up in the frame house my grandfather Patsy Borelli built on a narrow stretch of land between the mountain and Sinnemahoning Creek, pronounced crick. To a six-year-old this enchanted strip with the green-shingled homestead, springhouse, pig pen, woodshed and stream spells bliss.

My paternal grandparents, Maria and Thomas Costa, live a block away from us in Austin (although no one would think of measuring it in this fashion) at the head of Turner Street. My father's brothers, Dom, Frank and Joe, are already grown with families of their own. The attraction in Conrad, in addition to the setting and doting grandparents, are young aunts and an uncle. Madeline and Alfred are in their mid- teens and Louise, a mere 11 months older than I. Saturday morning and afternoon move slowly as we await our trip. Mom puts the baby, Sam Jr. down for a nap and begins to pack. She polishes our white shoes with a chalky-smelling whitener then puts them to dry on the porch railing. Dad comes home for lunch, hits the studio couch for 10 minutes to rest his aching arches, and returns to work. Thomasina and I play with the younger VanVolkenberg girls, Autumn and Fern, whose home backs up to our hill garden. Dad takes his supper break and this time Mom piles us in the car to take him back to work. Afterward there are baths, clean clothes and at 7:30

we get in the car, stop briefly at my Costa grandparents where Grandma doles out Hershey kisses. Back in the car we pass St. Augustine's Church and park just below it on Turner.

Opposite Gilroy's, we wait for Dad to close the store, Mom parking in Dad's usual spot under the first shady canopy on the maple-lined street.

Mom fishes out a quarter for Thomasina and me to go across the street to Hernquist's, the drug store at the west corner of Main, for ice cream cones. The freezer section of our refrigerator will hold a pint on special occasions, e.g. a birthday celebration, so this is a rare treat. As we start across the empty street, Mom calls, "Get a plain cone for Sonny," the family name for Sam Jr. I never tire of the astringent pharmaceutical smell from the back of the shop blending with the sweet aromas of the ice cream counter. We return to the car and Mom tsk tsks over the fact that "Doc" Hernquist has charged us two cents for Sam Jr.'s empty cone. Ours, filled with creamy vanilla, are 5 cents. Savoring the icy sweetness we play on the adjacent broad walks of the Community Center, Mom chatting with those who come by.

Ella Gilroy, wife of Bill, Dad's employer, is first. Her silver hair elegantly coiffed, she leans heavily on a cane after a visit to the hairdresser and admires Thom's black curls and my bangs which Mom has had permed to soften the long braids.

Just after nine, the lights go out in Gilroy's. Dad locks up and gets

behind the wheel of our blue Chevy.
Cross the bridge over Freeman's
Run, Sharp's garage on the left,
Higgins Brothers store on the right,
and head toward Costello.
Just before we get to Costello, there
is a farm on the right, a neat gray
house with a large barn. When we
make the trip during the day, Mom
stops to buy brown eggs.
 The farmer's wife has no nose, and
no prosthesis covers the twin holes
in her face. Mom warns me
beforehand not to stare, but my
gaze finds its target. The woman
gives no hint that she is aware of
the scrutiny.   Hens scratch in the
dirt at our feet as I ponder the
cause of her affliction, whether it
still hurts and if and how she
blows her nose.

. The long summer twilight is

coming to an end and so are the electric lines, the dim glow of kerosene lamps shining from the windows of the homes on either side of the road. We are nearing the site where the world's largest tannery once stood. It was Grandpa Costa's first place of employment in the new country, my father born on tannery row. There is scant evidence now that the spot had ever been anything but meadow. On the left upper hand side of the road before we reach the site is the home of Mrs. Fowler, mother to Elva Wolfanger, wife of Wormy(Laverne) who works with Dad at Gilroy's.

Mom took me there once to visit and inexplicably the image of a sunny kitchen, black and white tile on the floor, a copper teakettle on the stove imprints itself on my

mind. Below the house, the sun sparkles on Freeman Run soon to meet the Sinnemahoning at Wharton eventually flowing into the Susquehanna. We move on past the Protestant Cemetery, then the Catholic Cemetery high above us. There is no sign of St. Paul's Church which served the Catholics including my great-grandparents at the turn of the century.
. At Wharton we pass Charlie Peters' general store and take a sharp left on to the dirt mountain road, now only 10 miles from Conrad, all of it up. I know the names of most of the families, the houses few and far between. The Glovers have a swinging bridge; the Wykoffs, and Purdys are farther along. Go a distance and then the Casbeers, Fuzzy Bergland's place and the Commino's red house and

barn.

Dusk has turned to blackest night. Our headlights pick up the yellow eyes of wild animals, some of them behind the Susquehannnock State Forest fence, and I shiver with the pleasure of being scared and safe at the same time. It is the last and longest leg of the trip and should the Chevy run into trouble we would sit there until morning, or until Grandpa Borelli comes looking for us.

Then after what seems forever we are on the outskirts of Conrad, at the crest of the hill, on the upper bank the one room schoolhouse Mom, Madeline and Al attended and Louise still does. The Hunsingers live next to the school, Atkinsons across the road.

In the rear of the small white building are two rooms, quarters

*for Flossie Shields, the
schoolmistress and unofficially the
village social director. I can see
lights at the rear of the school
house and this is my cue to eagerly
peer through the window down
across the field and the crick to the
beloved, green- shingled house.
All is black, but as eyes adjust to
the darkness, I make out the dim
light of the kerosene lamp in the
window and picture it atop the
library table facing the stream.
"Hurry, hurry," is the prompt from
the back seat. Dad drives carefully
down the slight hill into what was
once the center of a booming,
logging town, all traces of the
industry long gone. On the left is
Indra and Florence Williams'
general store cum post office and
hotel, my grandparents' road
directly opposite, the Levi Gleason*

house on the right.

The East Fork road continues to Cherry Springs, the WildBoy (stream and road) on the left, opposite Walkers Hotel, a lone remnant of logging days. A sharp turn and we head toward the crick, past Grandpa's barn which houses Betsy and her calf Jackson. We approach the bridge, the shrill, deafening cries of the peepers abruptly stilled as the tires rumble across the wooden planks.

Directly ahead, Grandpa's black Chevy is housed in a tar-papered garage, backed up against the mountain and shaded by an ancient apple tree. In bloom, the fragrance permeates the air, mingling with that of the earthy scent of woods and the dampness of the creek. Little green apples will follow, capable of producing severe

stomach aches. Overhead the
moon's brightness is reflected on
the murmuring water.

Both doors opening onto the front
porch are ajar, faint streams of light
spilling onto the porch. Louise,
Madeline, Alfred, Grandpa and
Grandma are silhouetted in the twin
doorways of the living and dining
rooms. Then Grandpa is off the
porch coming to the car to help
carry us to the house, the grass wet
with heavy dew. Hugs and cries of
joy all around–especially if we have
missed a week or so.

The aroma of strong coffee
perking on the big, black
Kalamazoo wood stove and freshly
made fried cakes fills the
downstairs. We gather around the
big oval table in the dining room
and Grandma brings in the coffee
pot and thick china cups.

Louise has shaken some of the still warm donuts in brown paper bags with granulated sugar, some in powdered sugar, placing them in a blue enamel colander. Somebody discovers that Sam Jr. has crawled up to the dining room table and taken a bite out of each one while the rest of us are exchanging hugs. Coffee with lots of canned milk in it is allowed. I dunk a sugar-dusted fried cake in the milky, sweetened coffee, savoring the moistened bite before it falls into the cup. An audible yawn escapes, and Louise whispers to me, "Let's go upstairs. I have lots to tell you."

We scramble up the narrow steps to the back bedroom she shares with Madeline who goes before us with a kerosene lamp. Sloping ceilings and sprigged wallpaper await us, the two brown metal beds

covered with Gram's pieced quilts.
The lamp will remain on the
bureau as I am afraid of the dark,
circles shifting on the ceiling above.
I snuggle into the warmth of the
quilt, secure in this beloved haven
in the wilderness. Before Louise can
impart one confidence, I fall asleep,
mesmerized by the wavering light .
It will be many years before I
realize that not everyone is blessed
with hills and forest, mountain
streams , dirt roads, patchwork
quilts, and kerosene lamps. Nor do
I realize that a gossamer memory
has been woven this night, one
which will stay with me, and
despite its sketchiness, warm me
forever.
Eventually I will begin to ask
questions and learn the story of how
our great-grandparents and
grandparents, by choosing the wilds

of Pennsylvania, have bequeathed this cherished legacy, one for which they and others paid a high price. Cherry Springs, the Wild Boy(stream and road), Hammersley Station, Odin, Costello, Wharton, the Prouty, Keating Summit have transcended their place name status and become lyrical images that delight and entrance, evoking memories that make the heart leap and emotions soar more than a half century later.

"Albany Street Kid," and "Growing Up Italian in God's Country,"are available as Ebooks and in paperback from <u>Amazon.com</u> and from the authors. Email:<u>patcosta@rochester.rr.com.</u> for more information. www.patriciacostaviglucci.com

www.ingramcontent.com/pod-product-compliance
Lightning Source LLC
Chambersburg PA
CBHW060738050426
42449CB00008B/1260